PRAISE FOR

DO I BARK LIKE A DOG?

'A fascinating account of identity and belonging. Volpe writes with passion, insight and humour about his Italian family and his life in London. I loved it.'

JAMES HALL
Author of *The Industry of Human Happiness*

'In gloriously exuberant language Volpe lays bare the essential *him*... This is a man who has opera in his blood and knows how to move us with a master-director's artistry through a celebration of the value and delicacy of difference, which is often laugh-out-loud funny.'

DONALD MACLEOD
Writer and broadcaster

'A jaw-dropping tale – poignant, powerful, passionate and political. Fasten your psychological seat belt for a wild ride.'

KATHY LETTE
Author

'As with Puccini or Mascagni, his tragicomic tales of life as an "English" boy from Campanian stock are a spezzatino of laughter, shock, tears and irresistible pleasure.'

MARK VALENCIA
Opera critic

'At once tender and unflinching... this memoir is a song of self-discovery, celebrating the transformative power in remembering who we are. Michael Volpe demonstrates masterful storytelling with global resonance and local colour. This book will stay long in the memory.'

NITIN SAWHNEY
Composer and producer, Booker Prize judge

'A fine book. A love story really to identity. A treat.'

DANIEL FINKELSTEIN
Journalist and author of *Hitler, Stalin, Mum and Dad*

'While Brexit continues tearing apart the nation, Michael has been watching and commenting on what's been the needless tragedy of our times.'

CLARE COLVIN
Opera critic and author

DO I BARK LIKE A DOG?

Do I Bark Like a Dog?

How an Italian Family History
Shaped a Boy in London

MICHAEL VOLPE O.B.E.

RENARD PRESS

RENARD PRESS LTD

124 City Road
London EC1V 2NX
United Kingdom
info@renardpress.com
020 8050 2928

www.renardpress.com

Do I Bark Like a Dog? first published by Renard Press Ltd in 2024

Printed on FSC-accredited papers in the UK by 4edge Limited

Hardback ISBN: 978-1-80447-087-9
Paperback ISBN: 978-1-80447-086-2

9 8 7 6 5 4 3 2 1

CONTENTS

DO I BARK LIKE A DOG?

PROLOGO

I was born in Kensington in 1965. I grew up in Shepherd's Bush, on the streets and railway tracks of west London, the housing estates of Fulham, the terraces at Chelsea FC's Stamford Bridge, and at a remarkable English school at the bucolic end of Suffolk. I work in the world of opera, and Princess Anne pinned an OBE on my lapel at Windsor Castle, and yet, to this day, I *feel* one hundred per cent Italian.

How I perceive myself has always been framed by my immigrant family and childhood experiences, by the culture and language around me, the places where I spend time and the dramas and angst that seem so uniquely Mediterranean. This interpretation of myself seemed never to be just incidental or a mere oddity; it was more than that, and it is something I believe set me apart – I think it still does – although not in any particularly superior way.

That's a lie, actually. I did, at some point, believe it made me superior. When I was a child, the sense of otherness came through my knowledge of things beyond the experience of my friends, if only of culture, language, landscapes and food. These were profound topics to impose upon my playmates, and impose them I most certainly did. Ever since, people have asked me what I mean when I declare my cultural allegiance, but to be perfectly honest I don't have a ready or easy explanation.

As I grew through my teens and into adulthood, my Italianness sometimes met with hostility, racism or lazy stereotyping;

3

yet despite such incidents, my experience and demonstrable attachment to my cultural origins more often met with a positive glow. The boom in international travel meant that more people became Italophiles, and more and more would talk animatedly to me about their love of the place.

I identify with Italy and, although I have never made it my home, *at home* is what I feel whenever I visit the country, despite its myriad problems – a list of which would also fill a book.

The determination of others to criticise and upbraid me for feeling this way appears to be endless. 'You were born in England, so you are English,' they say.

Ironically, the fact that a person was born in the UK now appears to mean very little to some – and they don't actually think being born here means much if your skin isn't lily-white.

Instinctively, I find absurd the idea that my *place* of birth – the legal definition of my nationality – and the passport I hold define me *more* distinctly than the culture that nurtured me. Here I often meet with objections, because people believe the UK *did* nurture and educate me, and it was the UK that supported my immigrant family. None of this is untrue, but it doesn't change the way I feel about who I am. As it so happens, because my parents registered my birth in Italy, I *am* an Italian citizen, can vote in elections there and was even called up for military service, so I am legally an Italian, too. But, if I might paraphrase the quote attributed erroneously to the Duke of Wellington: 'If a man is born in a stable, does that make him a horse?'

Well, does it?

I first heard the quote when one of my uncles, who lives in the UK but is an inveterate Italian patriot, used it to insist that my brothers and I ought to consider ourselves, first and foremost, Italians. Actually, what he used to say was: 'If a horse is born in a stable, does it bark like a dog?' I have no idea where the dog came into it, but I knew what he meant. The original quote I have since seen appropriated by racists on the far right, so the question, particularly post-Brexit referendum, has begun to take on a more sinister undertone. But this was also a genetic argument – almost one about racial purity – that I am instinctively uncomfortable with. I don't feel as though I want to make an argument in favour of this dimension of the discussion, but cannot promise I won't go perilously close to it at times.

To be perfectly honest, I have always felt a little like a fish out of water in Britain, and I know many who feel the same. You cannot experience a life that has a dimension of rich, foreign family history (experiences, a different language, a name that singles you out) and not find yourself scrabbling for a sense of where you belong. It claws at you, digs you in the ribs and, in my case, makes me look at the British with the eye of an outsider.

And then came Brexit. What had been a lifelong philosophical imbalance for me became a bona fide reality as half of the UK decided any association with the country of my family was to be eschewed. Brexiters may tell you they feel animosity towards the institution of the EU, not towards Europeans, but it doesn't actually feel like that.

Nostalgia for my social and genetic history, those Italian family visits that were like character-plays, is packaged into parcels of memory: a home life and several holidays distinguished by our growth from small children into teenagers, and then into adults. It is a measure of either its potency or my emotional penury that my identity is based on what amounts to a few months' worth of experience in Italy as a child and as a young man. I would contend, however, that I had a reference point and persistent experiences that none of my friends in London had.

I can imagine there are countless people, from all races and religions, who feel the way I do about their cultural histories. Our everyday lives are here in the UK, where we experience everything the country has to offer, or is supposed to stand for. We go through the big events with those who consider themselves to be exclusively British – or English – but we don't always feel a part of it. When the Queen died, I looked at the whole extraordinary process without a patriotic eye, but I fully understood what she meant to the country. I saw a national performance I could admire, but not *feel*. This wasn't an anti-royalist position; the Queen had figured large in my life, just as she had in everybody else's. My mother was fascinated by the royals, and I was never taught to hate them, yet I don't have a *pride* in them as English people do. The Queen's death created a strange feeling in the country, similar to its reaction to the death of Princess Diana. Indeed, although that event had an inherently shocking impact on most people, including me, it was the strangeness of its aftermath that most struck me. Working close to Kensington Palace at the time, I wandered along to the gardens, completely bewildered by the scale of the automaton mourning, thousands of people quietly emerging from the tube and walking silently, flowers in hand, towards the palace. I felt like an observer, griefless, outside of the loop, watching this display and seeing the ocean of blooms running all the way from the palace to Kensington High Street.

In the context of Diana's death, it all struck me as a peculiarly British display of guilt, but I was aware of how the soap opera of the royal family has always provided a strong sense of identity for the nation. Wandering the edge of the flower-line with a couple of colleagues, we all gently laughed at a comment one of us had made, and were instantly set upon by a furious passer-by who believed we were being disrespectful. It wasn't the moment to go toe-to-toe with the mourner over what a lot of people saw as the hypocrisy of the grief, but, if I am honest, I didn't feel it was my place to point it out anyway.

There are countless examples of this disconnect, of a lack of 'affinity', but while I admire much about the UK, the things for which British people feel pride I do not share in, because pride is a possessive concept. I'll avoid the philosophical oddity of feeling proud of things your accident of birth had no role in creating – like beautiful countryside – but I sense the UK is itself setting fire to many of the societal qualities that once distinguished the country. At the new King's coronation, republican protestors were arrested before they'd even done any protesting, which ignited a blaze of objection on social media from people concerned at the authoritarian behaviour of the police. Others felt that to protest at such a moment (is there a better moment for an anti-monarchist to protest?) was robbing the public of their enjoyment of the day. Nevertheless, many of us, including royalists, were gravely concerned at the curtailing of an inalienable right Britain had done so much to defend over the years, and at which other countries gazed longingly. It appears that England, in particular, is having a crisis of identity which in turn is fanning the flames of mine.

I have always just accepted a lifetime of discombobulation as an inevitable consequence of my Italian origins. Until now, it hadn't become the meaning of life, nor had it ever truly punctured my sense of security; not feeling 'at home' in the UK wasn't critical. It was just *there*, and I didn't spend my time being angry about it.

I'm in my fifties, and yet my family origins still resonate with me; in fact, the history becomes more important with age. Curiously, as I write, the splendid American actor Stanley Tucci is all over the media with his recollections of his Italian family, projecting his memories through the prism of food. It all seems so lovely, but there is little that is benign about my lot or the life stories that emerge. There will be no food recipes in this volume (although food will pop up from time to time).

I am spilling my beans as I go along, so whatever gets there first gets on the page. I realise I have had a strange and dramatic life when all is said and done, but understanding its origins and its importance to my character and mentality is what made me sit down to write this book. When I told my brother Sergio about this project, he said, 'It sounds like therapy.' He could be right. I'll be perfectly frank and say there are things I don't think will make it to the page; there are people who would not want me to tell their entire stories because of the pain it would cause.

People have, though, asked me what this book is about, and I suppose that may well be something best decided by the reader. It is memoir of a fashion, a family history and a journey of self-exploration, tying together the experiences of people decades ago and discovering their impact on the life of a boy in London. Any point that may emerge by the final page will presumably percolate to the surface, just like the coffee in the little silver stove-top pot my mother used, but the story I tell might prove more interesting and important than any part I play in it. The tales I tell, and their implications, cascade down through the generations, landing at my feet. Throughout my life I have chosen to pick up the pieces and fit them into my own puzzle.

One final thing: this is how I remember it. If you have evidence to the contrary, keep it to yourself.

CHANGING TIMES

It is a simple truth that my affiliation with people and places twelve hundred miles from London runs deep. It is important to remember that the vast majority of my (large) close extended family live in Italy, and they have their own memories and a sense of ownership of the exotic, too. But a 2016 trip to Montecorvino, my parents' home town, close to Salerno, proved to be as profoundly revealing as any I had experienced before, and what characterised it was the *normality* of the dysfunction I encountered, the fracturing of families I remembered as being loudly and dynamically united and the unveiling of a side to Italy that, despite its occasional ugliness, has done little to diminish my desire to identify with the place, warts and all.

It was also my first visit to the family seat without my mother, whose death two years prior, along with that of my brother Matteo, framed the visit in ways I should have expected, but which still set trip wires for me to stumble over. I had not kept in touch with much of my family in the years since my last visit in 2004, but Facebook had brought me back into contact with cousins I had once been close to and, indeed, with *their* children.

Mum's absence was difficult to bear because these were the places I so explicitly associated with her and her history. I had to dredge the Italian language from the depths of my memory (or perhaps my soul?) but, more specifically, I was calling forth the dialect my family speaks at great velocity, and there was no Mum to fill in the gaps or to translate the more colourful, acrobatic passages. I was soon engaging in arguments with a fluency I would prefer to be more refined but was nevertheless grateful for. Neapolitan dialect doesn't bother much with verbs, which means you can be as inaccurate as you like and nobody notices.

Arriving at Naples airport and driving to Montecorvino always makes me feel a little anxious. The traits of southern Italians that can send a person insane include the way they drive, but in general terms Naples is the capital city of a place called Dontgiveafuckville. And Neapolitans remain the most creatively manipulative population on the planet.

I could give you several stories, told to me by Mum, of spectacularly brazen cons played by Neapolitans. My favourite is probably the chaps selling expensive televisions from the back of a lorry, raking in the cash quickly and handing people their heavy sealed boxes, which, when excitedly opened at home, contained the empty shell of a large TV full of nothing but newspapers.

The car hire at the airport is a good example of simple Neapolitan trading logic. The hire centre is five hundred yards from the airport terminal building, and you could walk there, dragging your bags in the pitiless heat along precarious and pedestrian-unfriendly roads, or you could take the shuttle bus from the car park opposite, which is still a dangerous feat to reach. If you choose the bus option, you discover that the shuttle is a small minibus driven by a man who loathes his job – and probably you, too – and you are fortieth in the queue. However, there *are* helpful taxi drivers nearby, who are prepared to take you the five hundred yards for a crisp ten-euro note, and your first thought should be that the car-hire companies' staff are getting a kickback from the cabbies – because that is the way it works in Naples. The logic is that nothing in life is, or should be, entirely free unless you are prepared to suffer (as here, wait an hour to go five hundred yards), so you make life a little easier by paying. They have this philosophy down to a fine art, and you can't help but admire them, despite your initial irritation. There is nobody to complain to, either, and if there were, they would have the ready answer that you could just as easily have waited for the helpful and generously free shuttle service. 'What's the matter with you?'

In Naples, you are never the cat who gets the cream, but they can make you feel as though you are as you gleefully hand over the ten euros, thinking you have beaten the system.

My first port of call was Lucio, the second-born son of Isidoro, my mother's elder brother, but it became quickly apparent that any hopes of a large family reunion would be dashed on the rocks of siblingly enmity. Lucio, a baker for as long as I can remember, is still working from his factory in Macchia, and his small but vibrant business, Iperpan, has made a name for itself, and is well known throughout the region. He specialises in the dried, aniseed-tinged *pane biscottato* that are soaked in water before being broken into rough lumps to be mixed through a tomato salad or to mop up sauce. His bakery has above it a large house that is divided into apartments for him and his children Ivo and Anna Maria, both of whom work at the hot ovens alongside him. Lucio, though, had ended his relationships with his siblings; I have never found out what exactly precipitated this state of affairs, and I'm sure if I did there would be several versions.

It was at his insistence that I had visited Lucio on the first day of my trip.

'What time do you arrive?' he said on the telephone.

'Midday,' I answered.

'OK, my house, two o'clock,' he demanded.

He remains as emotional and warm-hearted as I remember him to be, but a note of cynicism has emerged – or perhaps it's sadness? He works hard, from 4 a.m. each day, and his hands and thumbs are painful from working tonnes of dough over decades. Machines do much of that work now, but he reminds me of his father Isidoro as he sits at the table on his balcony, occasionally drifting off into private thought.

'You must come and see us every day and have lunch,' he said, not really considering that holidays these days had other pleasures in which to indulge oneself. But I had lunch with him for three days, and, despite the chasms between my previously close family members, I still had other cousins with whom a meal was insisted upon. Eventually, across the period of a week, I spent time with five of the fourteen children born to my mother's siblings – but the realisation that I possibly won't ever see those estranged cousins again was exquisitely sad.

The romanticised view I had of this corner of Italy has now changed. The beautiful landscape still strikes hard, even though modernity has arrived, along with growing towns and a knowing tourist industry. Yet what had always been pastoral, quaint poverty now just feels like the rapacious grasp of twenty-first-century inequality – and southern Italians drift between complete apathy and seething resentment according to the day of the week.

None of my family are living in centuries-old houses in imposing, high-sided cobbled streets any more, but in architecturally functional apartments. Visiting my cousin Nunzia on the edge of Battipaglia had a certain feel of danger to it, and although the gated estate in which they live might at first appear to be an accoutrement of affluence, it felt as though the electronic fences and doors were necessary to bar the way of a beast.

Public housing or not, the staggering vista from their balcony offers a full panoramic image of the mountains behind the town, craggy peaks from horizon to horizon, jutting up from the plain, with the sun waiting to plunge behind them. On their slopes you can follow the chain of villages from Montecorvino Pugliano, where my mother was born, down through Montecorvino Rovella, my father's birthplace, and then upwards again to Acerno. The roaring concrete serpent of the E45 *autostrada* that thunders past just a few hundred metres in front of us is the dividing line between the gloriously comforting past and the threatening present. Walking through the kitchen door on to that balcony and seeing that vision was as affecting as anything I was to experience on my trip. To Nunzia and her family, this was a daily sight, but for me it was like seeing a tapestry of my youthful memory, a landscape painting of my history; and from that distance, *nothing* had changed.

Standing beside me on the balcony, Marco, Nunzia's husband, was perplexed by my apparent speechlessness. 'Wow,' I repeated. 'Just wow.' He wouldn't have known that I was tracing the road between the villages and remembering how I used to ride the route on a scooter, nor what it meant to me to arrive at the top and look back on to the very position where we were standing, miles away. He probably didn't know the stories I knew of my mother's youth, or of wartime, the things that happened in those villages, even though a mile away was a British war cemetery filled with men who landed at Salerno. He would not have known how that view represented whole lives lived and now lost, families once united but now divided. He wouldn't have understood why I couldn't speak or swallow or stop the tears.

My cousins were keen to wallow in nostalgia, too. Lidia, Nunzia's younger sister, named after my mother – both of them, along with their youngest sister Ines and brother Ferruccio, are the children of Rolando, my uncle and one-time circus performer – loved to reminisce about our time as kids and our summer visits.

'I used to wait excitedly for you all to come in the summers,' she said. 'I always remember how Zia Lidia would arrive with a suitcase filled with clothes for all of us. It was like having another Christmas.'

Before making her annual trip, Mum used to spend days in North End Road market buying cheap T-shirts, sweaters and dresses for her relatives. An entire suitcase was filled with them, many of them weirdly inappropriate (vests with peculiar graphics were Rolando's favourite), but she was, in her mind, looking after her family, who she knew had little money for new clothes. All of my cousins on this trip were enormously emotional about the loss of Mum and wanted to talk about her. And they also wanted to talk about Matt, my late and frequently miscreant brother, whom they all appeared to have adored. Matt had gone to live in Montecorvino at about the age of seventeen – a desperate attempt by Mum to get him away from bad influences in London. The fact that Matt quickly attracted the local delinquents did nothing to diminish the affectionate memories of him my cousins wanted to share, somewhat painfully, with me.

'He was beautiful, your brother. Everybody loved him,' they would say tearfully, but when they saw how it affected me, they would rush apologetically to close down the conversation, as though guilty for having evoked the memory. It happened again and again throughout the visit, and it was exhausting. I was struck by the affection for Matt because it would have been some thirty years since he had last been to Italy, and so my family were, like me, holding on to romantic memories of distant, exotic relatives. They never got to see where his life took him, the physical peaks and troughs and the eventual irreversible decline of his drug addiction, nor his prison time, his utter chaos. I don't think that is a bad thing – I try not to remember that version of him.

It was Zio Rolando and his family with whom we spent most of our time as kids in Italy. their ancient little house in the backstreets of Nuvola, on the edge of Montecorvino, had pig sties beneath it and thick stone walls. Like London, and my first slum home there, these old relics have been demolished or converted into fancy homes, their original poverty-stricken residents moved on to charmless, crumbling modernity. Rolando's children were fiery, and Rolando didn't spend a lot of his time trying to manage them. I spoke a great deal in my book *Noisy at the Wrong Times* about Rolando, the circus performer and mushroom collector, the brother Mum most adored. It was Rolando who seemed to epitomise my own Italianness when I expressed it to my friends as a youngster, because despite his almost peasant-like demeanour, he had about him a veneer of Big Top glamour and superhuman strength. He was impossibly handsome, too, fantastically unique and funny, with a brilliantly expressive way of telling stories. His warm heart was the icing on this rich cake; I spent much of this trip hearing stories of him from his children, some of them much darker than I had imagined.

Italian families – in the south, at least – revel in history and past events, enjoying the conspiratorial elements more than any, embellishing and speculating to a point where you simply don't know whose version of a story to believe. My cousin Nunzia – whose physical similarities to Mum are striking – occupies the throne in this regard, sitting in the middle of a group gossiping and reeling off tales of misdemeanour, most of which appear to be laced with a little invention and which bring frequent admonishment from her son, Vittorio:

'Mamma! You can't say that. That isn't what happened!'

Nunzia would plough on regardless.

I had heard from my own mother the story of Rolando's short spell in prison back in the 1950s. He had been on a public bus that had pulled into the main square in Montecorvino, and the bus driver, for one reason or another, had offended a woman passenger. Rolando had taken issue. The driver then insulted Rolando and promptly shut the door, thinking himself safe, so Rolando took a seat at a café, supposing the driver would have to get off at some point since it was the end of the line. Noticing Rolando waiting, the driver stayed put, so eventually Rolando put his fist through the glass of the door and gave him a good hiding.

However, in Nunzia's version, the story came to include the use of a knife, which Rolando had allegedly plunged into the driver's thigh (it wouldn't kill him there). It occurs to me that Mum may have spared me the nastiest aspect of the altercation and that Nunzia was telling the truth, but it is impossible to know. The fact that Rolando had punched out the side of a bus was something of a legend in the town by all accounts, and I remember thinking it hugely impressive when Mum first told me about it. Whether he went to jail for the beating or a stabbing I am still unsure.

One evening, Rolando's children, together around the dinner table, revealed one lie (or a trimmed truth) my mother had told me about my uncle. His glamorous life as a circus performer had begun, we had always been told, as a teenager when he was 'discovered' larking about near the circus tent with his friends. The owner had spotted his acrobatic prowess and had asked my grandparents if he could take Rolando and train him. Mum told us that her parents had refused, but Rolando ran away with them anyway.

What was certainly true was that Rolando had become a minor celebrity and a real star of the trapeze, but the story had allegedly begun in his tenth year, when my grandparents, dirt poor and desperate, had agreed for him to join the Circo Fratelli Zavatta for a regular stipend. My mind cannot bear to contemplate what happened to him as a child; his heavy drinking and frequent desire for solitude in later life may have been telling a story of its own. My mother's need to prolong the lie and the bitterness she preserved in the memory of her parents suggests she never forgave them for it. She adored Rolando.

It was because of these stories and memories that I was especially keen to see Ferruccio, Rolando's only son and my cousin, whom I had last seen over thirty-five years ago. In that period, Ferruccio had spent eight years in jail for activities whose nature nobody wanted to share in detail. I didn't know what to expect. He had always been a mischievous, loud character, but how had he matured?

'Mike, when you see him,' Lidia said, 'you will think he is my father.'

He had now moved up the mountain and was living in Giffoni with his new wife and an eleven-month-old child, Ines, named after his sister. As a carpenter, he works fitfully when work is available on building sites, he is settled and is doing right by his family. I wasn't prepared, however, for the shock (and yes, emotional impact) of seeing him again. He was, as Lidia had reported, the image of his father at the same age; not as muscular, but he carried himself in the same way, his face was exactly the same, as were his mannerisms, voice and expression – even the way he sat with the back of his hand crooked to rest on his hip. And he smoked thin cigars just as his father had. I sat watching him, speechless at first, as though he were a reincarnation. Almost immediately, he asked me for photographs of my mother and brother Matt.

Of all my cousins, Ferruccio was the one I had seen least of over the years, so to see him for the first time since we were sixteen was powerful, but I wondered – perhaps I was even angry with myself – why our two lives had remained so parallel to each other. Why, if I was so emotionally connected to my Italian background, had I allowed it to remain an infrequent part of my adult life?

Marriage, careers and children intervene, for sure, but my eldest children, now into their twenties and thirties, have been to Montecorvino on only one occasion together. That was in 2004, when, before a full-length holiday in Sorrento, we visited Montecorvino. Knowing three days wouldn't be enough to visit all of my relatives, and that offence can be easily caused, we decided to host a large lunch for all of them at a restaurant. It was the first time I had ever seen members of my father's family in the same room as those of my mother. What was striking is that the Volpe clan was represented only by my then ninety-four-year-old grandmother, my aunt Anna-Maria – the only one of my father's siblings who hadn't left for England – and my cousin Tina, daughter of my Uncle Matteo, born and raised in England, who had married and gone back to live in Montecorvino. The Perillos had about fifty attendees. That event was also an emotional occasion, mainly because of the presence of my paternal grandmother who, with dementia enveloping her mind, didn't realise I was her grandson but exclaimed, on seeing me, that I looked like her son, Francesco. I remember that I promised myself I would visit more, keep in touch, but I didn't, and my children never asked to go again.

Now, twelve years later, sitting opposite Ferruccio, I began to wonder if a consistent relationship between me and my family might have changed aspects of my life. Or theirs. These meetings were becoming so pungently nostalgic that it began to confuse me, and I remembered how as a youngster I used to really love my cousins, and how they in turn loved us. I invited Lucio, Nunzia, Lidia, Ferruccio and their families to lunch at the farmhouse hotel at which we were staying. It was, in fact, the first time the cousins had been together for years, and we had a good meal, wine and grappa on the terrace – a family occasion they rarely enjoy these days, it seems. We reminisced, and Ferruccio and I implored Lucio to repair his relationships with his siblings as we argued and remonstrated. At one point, Lidia noisily drew the whole table's attention to me and announced, 'Mike looks happy!'

She was right.

AWAKENINGS

Ciucciarella inzuccherata
quant'è lunga sta nottata.
Fai la ninna, fai la nanna
che il tu babbo è alla campagna

Sweet little one
this night is so long.
Go to sleep, go to sleep
your father is in the countryside

These are the first words of Italian that I recall being aware of. They are from a lullaby sung to me by my mother as she stood at the side of the bunk beds that my brother Sergio and I shared in our damp basement bedroom. There were two sets of bunk beds – the other was shared by my brothers Matteo and Luigi – and in the middle of the room was Mum's large double bed, on to which we would launch ourselves from the wooden wardrobe in the corner of the room.

'Sing the song, Mamma, sing it!'

'*Fai la ninna, fai la nanna…*'

I didn't realise my bedtime lullaby was different from those of my nursery playmates, and I seemed to understand what Mum was singing, her voice heavy with Neapolitan dialect. It didn't seem odd to me that I had brothers with names that always stood out in a crowd, but my unusually English name was chosen by Luigi, who at the age of six, had already come to loathe his for the attention it brought him. Neither, for that matter, did I flinch at the taste of garlic, or the mounds of spaghetti we were served for dinner, nor find curious the rows of gnocchi on the kitchen table spread with flour, the gentle *canzone* of Sergio Bruni emanating from the sideboard gramophone as Mum toiled:

You weep only if no one sees,
and you cry out only if no one hears.

My mother spoke English with a strange accent, *and* she also had a strong Neapolitan inflection to her spoke Italian, but she was told to stop speaking the latter to me because I didn't appear to understand English as a toddler in nursery.

This was my world – one with loud relatives and family friends who would pack into the living room around a table whose edges were close to the tatty, torn wallpaper but left enough space to squeeze us all in. I enjoyed my daily job of grinding coffee beans in the little Dalek-shaped machine, down by the electric fire where the mice scurried, at the only power point in the room, and I remember screaming one day as a drawing pin was plunged into my knee. We went to hospital to have it removed because Mum couldn't face doing it herself.

The smell of coffee was ever present, along with the sound of gurgling stove-top percolators, brought steaming to the table on a tray with a miscellany of small clay *tazze*, painted with scenes of Paestum and Vesuvius.

'Let me put the sugar in, Zio!'

Now, who would give me their amaretti biscuit?

Our house was always full of life, a volume of complex, emotional dialogue with undulating lyricism and rat-a-tat speed. And hands would wave and gesticulate, something for me to mimic as I clashed with my brothers or my friends. I knew when they were swearing, too; the presence of children was no reason to stop.

'*Fa fancul' a mamat'!*'

These are not romantic inventions of my imagination. They happened, daily, in Woodstock Grove, Shepherd's Bush, as a group of exiles gathered, a simulacrum of the old country in a two-room slum, made habitable by inventive make-do, graft and wire wool in the cracks and creases of its cold, crumbling stone. Mum would scrub away at the floors and walls, as if bleach and endeavour would wash away the squalor; but there was warmth and colour – in music, language and food – and it was rich with the aromas of southern Italy. My family and other Italians who had come to London clung together, as all immigrant communities do, forming a critical mass to fend off the hardships of late-1960s London, aliens in what must have felt like another world.

It was all I knew. It was the air that I breathed.

My earliest memory is of my mother and me standing at the side of a bed in which a pale, gaunt man was sunken into the mattress with scarcely a flicker of life in him. The man smiled with effort and slowly reached out a hand, in which I saw a small foil-wrapped sweet. I took it and stared at him. I looked up, and, even in the darkened room, I could see my mother was crying.

Mum is crying in so many of my recollections of her.

The man was my grandfather, Nicola Perillo, and this was our first and last experience of each other. Word had come that he was dying and that Mum should hasten to his bedside. I was only two or three years old, so Mum had no choice but to take me with her on the long train journey to Italy, leaving her three other sons in the care of the Tully family a few doors along.

I remember nothing else of the trip – it is as though my unconscious mind recognised the significance of the moment in that room and awoke to record a snapshot of grief. I can describe the painted wooden cross on the wall above his head, the shutters that brought darkness to the room and the height of the ceiling, which seemed to tower above us like a cathedral.

I remember the smell, too: like sweet butter. I have only one photograph of my maternal grandfather, from the wedding of my mother's youngest sibling, Ines. In a ramshackle archway outside their home, a group stands as children sit on a step looking longingly at the bride, and my grandfather is at the edge of the group in a shabby, stained suit that is far too big for his slender frame, already reduced and shrivelling from disease. I can't help noticing that the three-button jacket is correctly fastened, by just the middle button. This was a man who fought for the Mussolini fascists, but he looks beaten down, haggard and not ferocious at all.

Even though her father was a hard, unforgiving alcoholic by the time of his death, Mum's grief was profound. The demise of her mother, Anna, several years later, was too swift for Mum to be able to return in time, and I came home from school to find her making pasta and weeping.

'My mamma is gone,' she said.

I was about eight years old. She had no husband to support her, and I was the first home from school, so it was my job to comfort her and be the first person to share her news with. Even as a child I recognised the gravity and the finality of her parental loss, and while I didn't grieve for a grandparent I barely knew, I felt Mum's pain. And her guilt for not having been with her.

I often think of my first trip to Italy and how Mum must have felt to trudge with a toddler through the village of her birth, to be at the side of a dying patriarch who, along with her four siblings and mother, she had left in order to escape poverty and chaos. Accompanied as she was at the time of her flight by a husband who specialised in capriciousness and deceit, she didn't escape it entirely, but she'd at least removed the risk of cholera, and her poverty wasn't nearly as grinding as that of her family back home. For me, the child at her side, the visceral image that remained – as clear as any memory I have – was like the opening credits of a film: a journey of identity was beginning, my cultural reference points staked out for me to follow and explore in future. I was there, in Pugliano, scarcely out of nappies, in a place of ancient history and heat. My earliest memories of Italy would be associated with death, but that trip is part of my tale, part of me and part of what I would become. I know that place, and returned there many times to add my story to that of my relatives, who knew nothing of our home in London, but whose lives would intertwine with ours for a few weeks. There were two worlds of which I was a part.

THE DEVIL IS IN THE DETAIL

As I grew up, I began to understand that this 'other' world, this Italian dimension, was distinct from my school life, the estate where we lived or my friends' houses. It had a depth and texture that is often excised from the toy-box characterisations of Italy we see in popular culture – we all know the stereotypes.

My experience, and why I feel the way I do, emerges from things more granular and full-blooded than the standard representations of Italy. With social media has come the ability to create beautiful vignettes – or 'reels' – of the landscape and the food that have a spangly authenticity but are ultimately just glamorous caricatures. Somewhat irritating but, I suppose, well meaning, are the TV programmes that dispatch a celebrity chef or actor to discover the Italian dream. As I write, a new BBC series has launched that puts Clive Myrie, the popular journalist and presenter and self-confessed Italophile, into a red Fiat Cinquecento (groan) and takes us from region to region, blending in Bond-movie locations and the usual magazine-style interviews with peculiar or outstanding locals. He even gets to meet the Sicilian villagers who took part in the second *Godfather* film. Another series has also been announced in which Judge Rinder and Rylan Clark do the same. It is hard to keep up. It's all a bit Disneyland, and I'm never quite sure what these formulaic, clichéd programmes are hoping to achieve, above and beyond being travelogues. I may have missed them, but I have yet to see programmes that explore the social history of Italy, warts and all.

Among the immeasurable number of Instagram accounts dedicated to Italian food, there is a cook who rhythmically slops pasta around a large pan, intoning his catchphrase that this is 'the sound of love' (misaphobics should avoid this one), and a sandwich shop that piles meats and cheeses on to ciabatta bread in a display of gargantuan generosity and *la dolce vita*. There are drone-filmed snippets of gorgeous coves in unknown parts of Italy, fashion accounts about Italian style, accounts that celebrate (or lampoon) the hysterical rantings of an unseen woman – on it goes, and it all acts as quite an overwhelming caricature of the country. In truth, it is just more stereotyping – stylishly done, but not a million miles away from the old Cornetto TV ads. Having said that, I could have done with Instagram in 1975 while I regaled my friends in the playground with stories of Italy and how great it was.

I look at this stuff with a suspicious eye, but beyond the superficiality of it and that intensely annoying chef with his sexualised pasta, it doesn't especially bother me. Indeed, it sings the praises of Italy above all else, salutes it, which is also what Stanley Tucci's book and TV programmes do. And I suppose it informs – or plays to – the reality I discuss in the next chapter, about the stereotyped Italy. Despite a recognition of the things these stereotypes represent, my conscious and unconscious sense of belonging is fundamentally formed by things I find it difficult to articulate: feelings and sensory stimulations, small rituals, gestures, atmosphere, behaviours and methodologies. We could take, by way of example, the preparation and experience of a meal.

It would begin with the shopping on Saturday, because Sunday was usually the day for the more epic meals, when perhaps we would have a get-together or celebrate a birthday. Mum would take her shopping trolley, order me to accompany her and march the length of North End Road market looking for the ingredients. In the 1970s, Italian delicatessens were actually more common than they are now, so specialist products such as exceptional pasta, dried tomatoes, dried fagioli, cured meats and the like were not expensive or difficult to find. Nowadays, a visit to somewhere like Camisa in Soho feels like a costly treat (and supermarkets have lots of products, which helped kill off many of the delis), but I recall an elaborate deli opposite the police station near Fulham Broadway in about 1974. It smelled so glorious I would sometimes just open its door as I passed it on the way home from school and take a deep sniff.

Finding vegetables was a bit of a minefield because few of the barrow boys were happy to see Mum pick up, feel and smell the produce. Most were rude to her, and she told each and every one of them to 'fuggoff' when it happened. In later years, Matt, Sergio and I all ended up working on the barrows and knew the people who owned them, so Mum eventually received preferential treatment. Once she had found what she wanted, the next stop was the butcher, to get her pork or chicken fillets for cotoletta or her beef for braciole, pork cheek for pasta fagioli, mince for polpetto. Salsiccia she could get from the deli, along with good olive oil, pasta flour (if she fancied making her own), passata di pomodoro and various cheeses. I followed her throughout all of this, understanding what meals she was constructing in her head, and I knew that none of my friends would be eating in the same way.

For larger meals, the preparation would begin almost the moment we arrived home and unpacked the goods. It was usually my task to tenderise the beef for the braciole, whacking the butterflied flank steak with a meat hammer, then to do the same to chicken or pork fillets – sometimes we would have both – but because Mum tended to buy lots of her utensils from the cheap barrows in the market, they wouldn't last long. If the hammerhead flew off, a rolling pin would do. Mum would begin the sauce for the braciole, which took several hours to make, and the moment the onions and garlic hit the hot oil, the process was truly underway, the aromas filling the kitchen, then the whole flat. Letting it sit overnight and then re-simmering gave the sauce a greater richness, and the braciole, now rolled and stuffed with garlic, parsley and parmesan cheese, would be dropped in on Sunday morning to cook for as long as possible. The smell of the braciole sauce, having permeated the house for twenty-four hours, would waft out of the flat and along the balcony, and our neighbours would shout through the kitchen window to Mum, 'Ooh, what are you cooking in there, Lidia?! Can we 'ave some?!' Frequently, Mum *would* parcel some up in a Tupperware box and deliver it to a neighbour, or she might boil up a small portion of penne, ladle out a dollop of the sauce, still bubbling gently on the stove, and tell me to deliver it to the young mum next door to feed to her toddler. Everybody who lived in the vicinity of our flat in Fulham Court will recall the smells that emanated from our house.

Pasta-making was arduous if there were a lot of people due to come to lunch, or it might be gnocchi, when my job was to rib the freshly prepared nuggets with a fork, sometimes overdoing it and squishing them into a small pancake that looked like a patch of corduroy. A house speciality was pasta fagioli, with pork cheek and, in her Montecorvino version, passata, potato and other vegetables. Beans for this – borlotti, cannellini too, perhaps – had to be soaked on Saturday night and then cooked sufficiently in the morning.

In essence, I acted as Mum's sous-chef. I was a child, but I could confidently beat the eggs into which I would dip the chicken fillets and then flop them on to the large plate full of breadcrumbs, coating each side, ready to be fried later. I did the same with sliced aubergines, but they didn't need the breadcrumbs. We had a Zyliss auto chopper, which just required me to repeatedly plunge a bladed, spring-loaded shaft into the plastic container holding the ingredient, and in this way I could safely present Mum with finely chopped garlic, herbs, onions or carrots. I could stir, smash, hammer, plunge and dip my way around the kitchen like a pro, and I could, triumphantly, use the stove-top coffee pot (known as a Moka but which Mum's lot always just called a *macchina*) to make Mum coffee for sustenance. Once all in the kitchen was in place, it was time to rearrange the living room, pulling the large, round, two-leafed wooden table out into the centre of the room, opening it and then placing beside it a plastic collapsible table that Mum kept in the cupboard under the stairs. The tables were covered by a miscellany of ornamental tablecloths, fringed with embroidery and centred by cut-out patterns and metallic thread. I would then lay up the cutlery for maybe fourteen people (kids included), set the coasters with scenes from Sorrento printed on them, the glasses, condiments, cheap wine, grated cheese, water, Coca-Cola for the kids, and then push the sofas and the coffee table with its large glass ashtray further towards the windows to make more space. My final job was to vacuum the carpet, but if the wall-mounted phone rang, I might be told to go next door and ask if we could borrow two chairs because someone else had just announced to Mum on the phone that they would be popping over, which is 'a fucky pain in da ballocks!' Mum always cooked far more than was necessary to feed the attendees, but last-minute changes still threw her a bit. Now, with the house smelling divine and we hungry kids sneaking into the kitchen to tear off a bit of bread to dunk into the sauce, we wait.

The dynamics of the day were very much affected by the visitors we were expecting. Mum's best friend, Giovanna, whom she'd met in hospital when she was having me, would come with several of her children, which meant that only she and Mum would be chattering away in southern dialect (Giovanna was from Sorrento); the rest of the noise was from lots of children. If it was my Uncle Matteo and his wife, and often a couple of other Italians as well, the kids were drowned out.

That is also when I was more likely to just sit at the post-lunch table and watch them all talk and argue, when my brothers had usually drifted away and my cousins would be playing among themselves. I'd park myself at the table, listening to the conversation, sensing the inexorably tightening tension. It was at times like this when arguments formed into two distinct types, and even the soothing tones of Roberto Murolo on the radiogram could do nothing to divert the inevitable upset. If they were arguing about something trivial, the tone might still appear alarming to an outsider, but it was really just a conversation about the buses, or the council. The other type of row had something much edgier about it, and included startling crescendos of volume and intensity, with an exponential rise in the emphasis and nature of the hand gestures. This latter element is one of the most caricatured aspects of the Italian manner, and much mocked, too, but I am here to tell you that it is an art form, a dance and often quite beautiful to watch, even when Mum became upset and angry. While gesticulating, she might pick up a cup or knife, pepper mill or wine bottle, and wave it about, as though using it as an illustrative prop – 'He took my life and threw it in the dustbin' – with the prop representing her life. Usually, she slammed it down on to the table again in a final flourish. Immediately she had done this, everybody else would momentarily try to calm things down again before the return of the ferocious vehemence a minute or two later. These passages of burning disquiet were usually about my father, or grandfather, or they would be Mum taking my uncle to task for his traditional views. Through all of it, I sat still and transfixed at the table. It was operatic, balletic and frenetic.

It can't be so strange that these events have shaped me in a way that is profound and lasting. Is it logical that the world in which I grew up, a transplanted circus of pungent, Italianate vivacity, embroidered with shouting, misery, cruelty and suffering, is one I might value or define myself by? By the time I was old enough to understand the differences between my home life and that of my friends, I was lost to its potency, gathered up in its embrace and fully embarked on its dissemination to all who wanted to hear of its wonders or were drawn to its mystery.

I often wonder about this dichotomy and have a million questions, but I don't have many conclusions; if I had the answers already, my questions would be a waste of time. As the fifteenth-century Italian philosopher Giordano Bruno (which sounds like an operatic stage name) said: 'Time is the father of truth.' Plenty of time has now passed for me to make some sense of it or even find some truth, but it is worth pointing out that he also said, 'With luck on your side, you can do without brains.' If, as a master at my school, he'd said it about me, we'd be applauding his perspicacity.

Clever bloke, our Signor Bruno.

GIOIA!

THE STEREOTYPED ITALY

There are some nationalities that resonate powerfully – and not just negatively or disdainfully – with some British people. These cultures and countries are never fully denounced or vilified but are valued, admired and even absorbed to some degree. The French enjoy this privilege, although there is something of a schizophrenic approach to Francophilia in the UK. 'The bloody French' is a term never far from the lips of Brits as they buy up swathes of Provençal real estate, and it's still there after years living in the country. America is popular by and large, and a dream destination for many; they might drag us into wars occasionally, but there is that special relationship to think of. Scandinavians are admired, too, although not for their pickled fish and suicide rates. Germans are grudgingly respected, although never fully trusted, and Asian culture is generally seen through the blurred vision of a late-night curry or special fried rice. In essence, the world is viewed as 'them and us' by British people, but some get an easier ride.

In recent times, and especially since Brexit gave people permission to denigrate, mistrust and go to war on foreigners, the multicultural nature of the UK is often poked at by public figures who appear to spend their lives wanting everybody to hate each other – and as I write, this situation is getting worse and more explicit with every day.

My mother's generation were just the latest in a succession of waves of immigration from Italy, and Italians have a long, almost ancient affinity with Britain that has undergone more than one recalibration, particularly in 1940, when Benito sided with Adolf.

A potted history of Italians in the UK (and there are several hundred thousands of them) could arguably started with Julius Caesar sounding out the idea of colonisation in 54 BC with an expedition, landing in Kent. It wasn't until Emperor Claudius followed through in AD 43, invading and occupying the islands, that the process, which still today prompts me to tease the Brits that they are all Italian bastards, began in earnest. Don't @ me with 'But the Romans weren't Italians' – they made olive oil and wine and were gazing at the Bay of Naples when Vesuvius emptied its pyroclastic flow all over them.

Through the Middle Ages, Rome of a different hue was important to the British, with Alfred the Great getting his anointment from the Pope; and northern Italian bankers from Lucca and Florence were once the favoured money lenders to the British Crown.

Under the artsy Hanoverians, many Italian artists and musicians came over and flourished, and then (I'm skipping past Napoleon's wars, when thousands of northern Italian farmers, their lands destroyed, emigrated to the UK) we arrive at the Second World War. This was a tragic time, when Churchill ordered the police to 'Collar the lot!' once sides had been taken, and there was enormous hostility to Italians; thousands were rounded up and sent to camps. The choice Mussolini made horrified most Italians in the UK, who remembered the solidarity Britain and Italy shared during the First World War. In one deportation on the ship *Arandora Star*, four hundred and forty-six British Italians died when the ship was sunk by German torpedos. It was the desperation for labour in the 1950s that saw migration revive, and that was when my parents arrived.

So we've been here for a long time.

I conducted a piece of unscientific research in which I asked friends to give me one word that for them summed up Italy and Italian culture, and the first ten answers, in order, were these:

- Chaotic
- Food
- Life
- Opera
- Ice-cream

- Colour
- Barolo
- Riot police
- History
- Sun

I had asked for 'opera' to be excluded because so many of my friends enjoy or work in it, but obviously the significance was just too powerful for one individual. I had eighty responses to the survey, and food appeared many times, as did history and culture.

'WorsthotelIeverstayedininSanRemo' made me chortle.

'Riot police' came from a football friend.

'Quality' I loved.

'*Gioia!*' I loved even more.

One could conduct a survey like this on any country, but I would venture that few could produce so many responses that had a depth of feeling – and experience – quite like one on Italy. I like to think the answers from my circle of friends were dripping with affection. Apart from the one who said 'turncoats'.

That, of course, remains the black mark against Italy: the war and the Armistice that saw the country change sides. If I had a quid for every person I had punched in my youth for a reversing tank joke… Recent historical studies have sought to recalibrate that final year of the Second World War in Italy, the sacrifices of the people who were murdered in their tens of thousands as reprisal for resistance action, and the way it helped turn the tide of the war. Culturally speaking, though, it is mud that has resolutely stuck, and is for ever likely to do so.

The fact that Italy is famed for producing one of the longest-surviving fascist regimes in modern European history is part of the dichotomy of the country, which at other times has teetered on the brink of hard-line communism as well. It is a melange of regions and individual nations that were only relatively recently brought together as one country, and there is a cornucopia of languages and dialects. Officially, I think, there are thirty-four dialects in Italy, but in reality there are many, many more. In the south, these are labelled 'extreme dialects', and they can differ from one town or village to the next.

To this day, Italy remains divided emotionally, if not actually, between north and south. I was recently tweeted by a friend who was holidaying in Lake Garda: 'They fucking hate your lot up here,' he said. And curiously, even I feel that disconnect sometimes, believing the earthy southerners to be the 'real' Italians. Northerners would say I was welcome to such a view, because they call anything south of Rome 'Africa', and in some respects they are not entirely wrong historically, although they *are* being racist.

I have Cypriot friends who like to tell me 'All Italians are Greek bastards', but I point out that if I am the bastard child of anybody, he would likely be an Arab. The Moors (or Saracens) occupied Sicily and charged up the boot, leaving us with their tonal inflections in Neapolitan music, as well as their olive skin and black hair. If I discuss the hysterical nature of southerners in relation to this historical fact, I am in danger of racially profiling Arabs. So I won't. Instead, I will stereotype Catholicism, which rendered the south prejudiced, narrow-minded and hypocritical. The presence and power of the Church did nothing to curtail the capacity for viciousness that southern Italians possess, a trait best exemplified by the southern mafias – the Camorra and Ndrangheta – a key reason why northern Italians have such a distaste for their southern compatriots. In fact, the southern clans date back centuries, and they still spend most of their time arguing among themselves. Both Church and State are treated with suspicion in Italy, although the power of one (the Church) has gone some way to neutering the other; many Italians think democracy and its instruments are weak, so in response the institutions of State decided that infinite bureaucracy would lend them weight and authority. To Italians, bending the rules is another rite of passage.

The Mafia were a natural consequence of such an insubordinate people, filling the gaps that the State or Church left unfilled, because an organisation that represents the pinnacle of rule-circumvention is always likely to find fertile ground in which to set its roots. Ironically, many would argue that the Mafia has always been the most efficient government institution (and churches are full of Mafiosi).

In Italy, on our visits, I understood the lure of the Camorristi to the young men of Montecorvino. If truth be told, the Mafia have been romanticised by western culture, despite furious denials to the contrary. When Roberto Saviano's book *Gomorrah* was turned into a movie, people were able to see the depths of cruelty and stone-cold murderous depravity of the southern Mafia (who placed Saviano on a permanent hit list) but it was still turned into a TV series, avidly watched by millions, with characters the programme-makers clearly wanted us to give a shit about. If the *Godfather* films are the epitome of Mafia romanticism, honour and glamour, then *Gomorrah* is its feral, hack-and-slash child whose ghoulish awfulness we still appear to lap up. It is part of Italy, and it seems even the dark side receives a longing look and the shiver of a thrill.

I would be lying if I said I hadn't pressed this fascination into service as a youngster. Fulham had gangsters, some of whom we knew, but they were like the Salvation Army compared to the foot soldiers of Campania, who lure miscreant friends to country lanes in order to shoot them in the face so that they can't have open coffins. It is just business, after all; medieval in nature, but still just business. Even at primary-school age I was ready to expound the virtues of the Renaissance or Verdi as I understood them from my uncle's teachings, but it would frequently be the stories of murder and Mafia that got the greatest airing on the bus.

The savagery of the Mafia may seem an unhealthy occupation for growing minds, but you can imagine the currency it gave me in the snot-nosed underworld of the Addison Gardens playground. Being foreign in the early 1970s was still a moderately rare thing; I had a friend – Zoran – from Yugoslavia (as it still was then), and I remember him for always smelling of garlic. I probably did too, but if I could smell him over the organic mist of my own breath, he must have been eating it by the raw clove. There were Black kids, naturally, but to be white and of foreign stock was a relative novelty, and I believed, with childish certainty, that the stock to be was Italian.

Italy had so many pros, and even the cons could be turned into positives, or at least balanced up: for every reversing tank there was Sophia Loren and Gina Lollobrigida. We had great footballers playing for clubs glamorous beyond imagination, we had the best fashion, we had the Romans – who, at Addison Gardens Primary School, it was fervently pointed out, were in fact Italians – and we had cars, fast cars. Ferrari, Lamborghini and Maserati.

'My uncle's got one of those.'

'No he doesn't, you liar!'

'Who are you calling a liar? Do you know my uncle? Have you been to Italy?'

Who could argue with me? I stopped shy of saying that any of my family were in the Mafia, but I painted a romantic picture of them all because to me they were, and there was very little anybody could do to disprove my claims. I really did have an uncle who had become a star of the circus, of the high trapeze, and my playground activities would include swinging from rafters in the rain-shed to prove my genetic connection to him.

A FULL-SIZED ITALIAN AND

HOW I GOT THERE

'Volpe? The wolf!'

'No, actually, it means fox. It is the Italian word for fox. Lupo is the word for wolf.'

'I'm pretty certain it means wolf. That play, what was it? *Volpone!*'

'That was a play with characters named after animals. Volpone was the fox.'

'Oh, are you sure?'

'Yes.'

I can't tell you how many times I have had this conversation. Sometimes it goes a little differently: my interlocutor will say, 'Ah, the fox!' – and then, before I can congratulate them on getting it right, an onlooker will interrupt with, 'No! It means wolf.'

Even teachers at my schools did this to me, but it was just another of those small occurrences that made me feel different. I loved my name and its mystery. 'That's right, I'm not like *you*,' is what I thought it said, and I didn't really ponder why it was I cared about that.

I went to Woolverstone Hall – a boarding school – which meant there was a lot of time to interrogate the realities of each other's lives. Woolverstone was known as the Poor Man's Eton: it wasn't a posh, wealthy school, and most of us were from broken homes in London. We were just bright and

37

happened to get the chance to go to an unusual state school in the Suffolk countryside. But even at primary school it mattered to me that people understood who I thought I was, especially once I'd become fully aware of the differences myself. Wear my Italianness on my sleeve at Woolverstone posed certain risks, but they were risks I was prepared to take. Naturally, I spoke a lot about my family back in Italy, but a new dynamic emerged at boarding school that I'd not before encountered except on very rare occasions: racial abuse.

'Wop', 'dago' and 'greasy' were the top three. I responded with a threat of violence to all but the most benign versions from friends. A teacher once called me a 'spaghetti-eating Italian' in front of a whole class, who laughed heartily.

And then there were the reversing tanks gibes. Zzz.

Biff, bash, bosh.

Soon enough, people with hostile intent realised it was probably unwise to use my ethnicity to abuse me. *Admiration* for being Italian was most definitely not a thing at Woolverstone, so I just resorted to being a normal teenager and fought my way through school that way. But in school holidays, when we all hung out together back in London, the lavish meals Mum would force-feed my friends with struck a chord. That was me being Italian and showing an advantage on account of it. So I was forever seeing life through the prism of my cultural background. It mattered. At Mum's funeral I mentioned the meals she forced on people in her eulogy, and a knowing laugh rose up from the congregation.

My brother Sergio says he hated his Italianness for a period of his childhood because of the way people would talk to Mum – as though she were an idiot, with that ingrained, patronising disregard for foreigners manifesting in speaking slowly and in a loud voice. He was acutely aware that her English at that time was not perfect, and a visit to the post office or the bank would fill him with dread. 'I started finishing her sentences for her,' he recalls, 'so the person behind the counter wouldn't have the problem of not understanding and I wouldn't have that awful feeling when they spoke to her so disrespectfully.'

Sergio went to Woolverstone too, and also suffered abuse based on his ethnicity. One particular boy, two years above him, constantly referred to him as a wop, until one day Sergio, channelling that boiling fury we all seem to be partial to, set about him, first by smashing his face into his cornflakes bowl, and then by kicking him hither and yon around the dining room until he begged him to stop. Sergio was slippered by the housemaster for attacking a senior – this couldn't be tolerated – but the bully never called him a wop again. Along with our hurt pride, there was always a feeling that people might hate us for being Italian, and on reflection, this sensitivity was quite acute.

The violent reactions we had to racism may well have been less about the ethnic slur than the on-the-edge lives we'd had. You didn't *have* to call me a wop for me to think you were trying to assert some form of authority over me, and I recall a sense of threat in much of what I encountered, whether or not it *was* a real threat at all. Growing up on an estate where a lot of criminality occurred is something kids quite quickly absorb as normal, but this does create a hypersensitivity to people's motives towards you.

In Fulham Court there was a plethora of cultures, and we mixed well, but our family was linked through my brother Matt's lifestyle to the shadier side of west London, even though it was only *he* who came into direct conflict with the law. And naturally, we were known as an 'Italian' family. Many of Matt's friends were very fond of Mum, even though for some she reserved a laser-like suspicion, and she wouldn't be averse to giving them a good verbal going-over from time to time. Policemen who stopped me in the street for a casual search when I was a teen would know precisely who I was and simply couldn't countenance the idea that I might not be following in the footsteps of my brother. This used to anger me enormously, and when they told me to empty my pockets I'd truculently drop the things I'd dragged from them on to the floor.

'This isn't fucking *Starsky and Hutch*, sunshine. Pick 'em up!'

Matt's frequent delinquency would bring the police to our door regularly, and it was often the local Fulham CID, who the community felt to be the most corrupt squad in London at the time. A visit from them took two general forms. The first was a knock on the door to speak to Matt about something they suspected he may have been involved with, but usually they would find only Mum and his brothers at home. An officer once nonchalantly slid his arse over the arm of an armchair and sat himself down in the living room when asking Mum questions, a display of presumptive authority that made us kids wince.

'Who said you coulda fucky si'down?' Mum said, quick as a flash. 'And donna talk to me like Ima fucky stupid. I might be foreigner, but Ima no fucky stupid, OK?'

The officer leaped quickly from the chair, but I imagine the humiliation was registered. Mum hated the fact that the police were constantly at her door, and she was in no way approving of Matt's behaviour – it tormented her for decades – but she always knew when there was something to do with her nationality at play in an interaction, and gave not one single fig whether it came from a copper or not. If she suspected racism was at play when it came to her children she could be ferocious. I remember her angrily accusing teachers of being hostile to our ethnicity rather than our behaviour. Most of the time she would take a teacher's side, but from time to time her radar twitched.

The other form of local police engagement was their habit of simply kicking the door down at 6 a.m., hoping to catch Matt asleep. I lost count of how many times this happened, and it was always 'formative' for me. Standing bleary-eyed in my underpants at the top of the stairs, rudely awoken by the sound of coppers booting the door down must have been imprinted somewhere. I couldn't always assume they were police, either.

Once, they used both methods on the same visit. Unbeknownst to me, while I slept upstairs, they had knocked on the door and Sergio had opened it. Matt had been asleep on the sofa, and they all rather calmly agreed to go to the police station. They made an error, however, by walking out of the door ahead of Matt, who promptly shut the door, bolted it (yes, we had bolts) and began to escape up the stairs. Awoken by the sound of kicking at the door, I arrived on the landing as Matt rushed past, and looked down to see Sergio desperately trying to unfasten the bolts so the police wouldn't damage the frame. Sergio was screaming, 'All right! I'm opening the fucking door, don't kick it in!' as he pulled the final bolt, and with an almost cartoonish flourish three casually attired men, along with the splinters from the frame, came flying through the door, landing on top of a now prone Sergio.

That's when my befuddled brain told me they could be a different kind of villain, and I booted one of the policemen when he reached me on the stairs. He took it better than I expected. 'We're the fucking police! Get out of the way!' Obviously he had realised how it might all look. I could only have been about sixteen or seventeen at the time, so they didn't take too unkindly to me when they realised Matt had escaped like Spiderman on to the parapet and into a secret roof space in which he sometimes hid for many hours. He always eventually had to surrender.

It may seem strange to say it, but, apart from Matt, we were not an anti-police family – but we were anti-Fulham Police, and there wasn't a scintilla of trust in any legal process they might initiate; reports of falling down the stairs was common in the custody suite. Although Matt was usually bang to rights on what they were charging him with, more than once the police invented stories and charges that went all the way to court. I once sat through a two-day trial Matt underwent that contained so much fabrication and invention that the jury – and, as it turns out, the judge – saw right through it. When the jury had delivered a swift 'not guilty' verdict, the judge turned to Matt and invited him to press charges against the Fulham CID. Matt laughed at the idea and told the judge he had quite enough bad credit with Fulham CID without getting a couple of them banged up for falsifying evidence. I don't know why it became Matt's responsibility, anyway.

Reflecting on these elements in my life, it is probably fair to say that little of it had anything to do with my Italianness, although any subconscious resentments were undoubtedly wheedling their way into my behaviour. Essentially I was just a kid in a fish tank filled with piranhas – and acted accordingly.

When Matt died, his funeral and wake were attended by some faces from the old London gangs – quite scary people, in fact. They all seemed to love him, and several even mentioned his ethnicity warmly! Matt's villainy had always seemed fairly inconsequential, driven as much of it was by his addictions, but that dreadful day made me wonder how much of his life I had been ignorant of.

Growing from being a teenager surrounded by all this drama into adulthood – when the drama didn't ever really subside – my demeanour and awareness of how I wanted people to see me changed and grew, aided by any character that Woolverstone had managed to imbue me with. I knew, even at the start of my working life, that I would be prejudged for my inner-city bearing, and that is indeed how it turned out, but I understood that there was a character to be played, a method that would benefit me. *Italian* could also be a costume and a set of behaviours that I felt entirely natural enacting. It also sounds like a classic case of displacement. Even to this day I am aware of how some people, despite everything I might have achieved, too easily assume that actual dishonesty or potential criminality exists within me. I think this is more likely to come from the way I speak or carry myself than my Italianness, but it is a distinct prejudice nevertheless.

In my mid-twenties, I had the chutzpah to write a film script (titled *Ragazzi* – original, huh?) about a second-generation Italian, just like me, who employed a number of his friends as salesmen in a business he owned. The friends were an ethnic mix of African, Jewish and Irish descendants, and the primary condition of their employment was (because they would be selling to Italians and Italians only really trusted other Italians) that they would have to learn to *be* 'Italian'. I was playing with the concept of ethnicity – how we can adopt and appropriate characteristics – and the lead character was suggesting that by perfecting a few mannerisms, behaviours and ideas, anybody, even someone of African descent, could be accepted as one of 'us'. The lead character was, in fact, a racist. It is also obvious that I had my own suspicions about the potential vacuity of ethnic allegiance, as well as believing it was a place of safety for so many in a multicultural society. You could argue that to be an Italian in London, with Italian traits and behaviours, is in fact the epitome of being 'English' in the modern, multicultural UK. But the concept at play in the film script was that while a person can be anything they want to be, there will always be boundaries to what people will *accept* you as being. 'If you act like us, think like us, then we'll embrace you.'

There is a scene in the script in which the protagonist explains to his friends over a lavish Italian dinner what it means to be Italian. The speech talks about how to walk, talk, gesticulate, how to enter a room and assume everybody is looking at you while pretending you haven't noticed, how to wear a cheap suit and make it look expensive and so on. It was all rather cartoonish (some of it intentionally), but, in the words of the script, if they could master these things, they too could be accepted as Italian by other Italians. I actually believed that as entertainment it had legs, and whilst twenty-five years ago it would have seemed out of place, I can't help thinking that it would have a toxic relevance to how things have become today. But some of it is awful, and it shows how obsessively I was contemplating my self-image at the time. I wonder if I appeared weird to others.

It is indisputable that I was often, in the minds of others, defined by my ethnicity, and I worked it as much as I thought necessary. 'You are *so* Italian!' was – and remains – a common cry, and I suppose I *look* Italian, with my skin tone, hair and funny walk. I'd sometimes ask what was meant by 'You are so Italian', and the answers were a cornucopia of stereotypes, none of which I had a right to object to since I was so busy trying to make people notice them in the first place. It is also true that some of the things people consider to be revealing of my background really do exist unconsciously and without affectation: the use of hand gestures, volume, emphasis, an intensity of conversation and gaze that I think some can find challenging. Sometimes, just being loud did it, and that probably hasn't changed to this day.

It was when I was in my mid-twenties that I started to focus on the feeling of 'not belonging', or of being in limbo. I knew I didn't want to live in Italy – life had moved on and I was busy doing my thing, but I had always supported Italian national sporting teams – and drew a lot of criticism for it, too. I felt there was an arrogance about the English that I didn't identify with, and much of this was informed by the environment I encountered at football matches.

I had been going regularly to Chelsea since I was five years old, and either on my own or with Serge and other friends since the age of eleven. This was in the mid-to-late 1970s, when kids could just turn up and pay 50p at the turnstile, and racism, xenophobia and that one-dimensional tribal mentality – based not just on the colour of your club's shirt but on violence and gang-like warfare – was the prevailing mood.

It is really quite a challenge to articulate the feeling – discombobulated is how I describe it elsewhere – but I just did not feel at home here. Familiar, yes – comfortable, even; but like I belonged? No. I just didn't. I had friends, colleagues, acquaintances just like anybody else, and I didn't live in a box, separated from humanity or kindness. I was, it is fair to say, able to portray the Londoner I undoubtedly am in many respects, and this served a purpose in certain environments. I knew, however, that people saw me differently and that I could not always be sure their attitude to those differences was benign. Ultimately, I think I chose to draw down harder on my heritage, to use it to satisfy myself that I was different, and took on a boldness of characterisation as a shield. There was no way on earth I was going to pretend I wasn't from a foreign culture, so I exaggerated it and resolved to actively antagonise, via that exaggeration, anybody who gave me reason to mistrust them.

Those readers who share similar backgrounds to me, be it Italian or any other nation, will perhaps recognise what I am talking about – particularly the propensity to hyper-vigilance. Psychologists reading this might theorise that my connection to a far-off place was simply because that is where I best experienced the concept of 'happy' families. They might be right, but they would never convince me that the *location* of what I had an affinity with was entirely irrelevant. If you, dear reader, are English and see yourself through that lens, you ought to be able to empathise with the connection to one's culture, surely?

THE OPERATIC INDULGENCE

In 1989 I began a job that would lead to a thirty-three-year career in opera – an art form inextricably linked to Italy. Opera chose me, not the other way around, but the things that came to represent my place in the industry were most certainly a choice and, even more certainly, very much informed by my visceral connection to the Italy I perceived with great clarity. We are moving into 'nurture or nature' territory here.

Over those years, my London-based company, Opera Holland Park, became associated with a particular brand of opera: the Italian period of opera called '*Verismo*', or 'real life'. These were '*stab-and-sob*' operas – violent, passionate, catastrophic and musically overwrought at times. Their tortured strings, engorged with melody and tinged with Italian folk music, seemed to evoke a landscape and society I felt utterly familiar with. There is a kind of synaesthesia at play when I listen to them: cue the string intermezzo, here come the visions of mountains, the cacophony of washerwomen at the fountain, the whiff of wild herbs…

The plots of these operas usually include betrayal, love, desertion and violence, all of which felt very familiar, too. Stories of tortured mothers, despairing of their wayward sons, had a naturally profound impact on me; young, innocent front-of-house staff might approach me as I watched a show from the side, only to be thwarted by seeing me a hot mess of tears.

Not all of this was coincidence, surely? I'd suggest none of it was. One particular writer whom I regularly commissioned to deliver essays for our programmes would try to slip various outrages into his prose to test if I was paying attention and editing content diligently. In a discourse on *Werther*, he once dropped in the little bonbon, 'And like all Frenchmen, he was a homosexual.' Of course it was cut, but I expect if he had written 'And like all Italians, he was hysterical' it may have been allowed through.

Like many others, I first encountered some of these works through their use in films or advertisements. Even as a teenager I was instinctively drawn towards anything that had even a whiff of Italian origin, and when Martin Scorsese used the intermezzo from *Cavalleria rusticana* for the opening credits of his film *Raging Bull* in 1980, I was bewitched; the beautifully shot ballet of De Niro's shadow boxing juxtaposed with the weeping strings of Mascagni's music was perfectly judged. Composers like Mascagni were obsessed with creating music that was relentlessly picturesque, but wanted to set it to extremely violent, grim scenarios. Scorsese's film was doing that very thing, and of course, the soundscape is so evocative of Italy and was, perversely, exactly what a film about a violent, abusive Italian-American boxer required.

When we presented our first of these *giovane scuola* operas in 1997 – Mascagni's *Iris* – there was a real impact on the opera-going public. It was so popular that we revived it in the following year, and again it sold out. Oddly, it is a piece set in Japan, and is full of the kind of Japanoiserie that was so prevalent in the late nineteenth century, but it was unmistakably Italian, even with the undoubted influence of Wagner suffusing the piece. Above all, the success of *Iris* enabled me to press on with my ambition to bring more of the works that I had been privately listening to for years to the stage, thus reviving the popularity they once had. I wasn't on a conscious crusade to elevate these works as a salute to Italian cultural greatness – they just struck home with me.

There followed many years of exploration of the late Italian canon, and I think it is fair to say that Opera Holland Park became the pre-eminent company in the UK for this stuff. A season of opera might cover a variety of styles and repertoire, but every year, for me, the excitement always came with the rarity, the 'mad Italian' opera that we had chosen and which invariably provided the greatest challenges. They filled the singers with excitement, too, and many of our notable achievements as a company would arrive with these works. I felt very much at home in their sphere, listening nightly and sensing the crackle in the air that they created. We were doing something unusual and risky, but making a success of it, bringing a higher profile to Opera Holland Park and granting it a wider recognition as an important company. It was, though, a visceral and indulgent journey on my part.

It was of immense satisfaction for both me and James Clutton (my management partner) that audiences loved discovering these operas, and they would often be the first to sell out, growing in popularity but also garnering affection. I recall being contacted by Italian academics, recognising our championing of this important pillar of Italian culture, and I was once even invited to write a chapter for an Italian book on *Iris*. One of the great thrills for me, and I suspect also for James, was when, on the opening night of a new production of *Iris* in 2016, the Mascagni family themselves, including the composer's granddaughter Maria Teresa, attended and presented us with original photographs of the great man with personal inscriptions. Maria Teresa thanked us for our two-decade-long journey of producing – and thus exposing the British public to – various operas by her grandfather, a man she remembers spending time with as a small child.

I revelled in the contribution I was able to make to amplifying a particular facet of Italian culture, but it seems to me that the British audience we served found their own connection to the music and dramas that these operas represented. A journalist friend once interviewed Richard Attenborough and asked why he always made such emotional films, and he replied with, 'Every tear a dollar, love.' It is indeed true that opera audiences are besotted by a tragedy, a murder, a betrayal, a suicide or a heart broken by a love triangle, and these works have all of that in spades. When my life went through difficult periods, of grief or general unhappiness, these works became painful reflections of my travails, and some evenings at the theatre were especially difficult. Art is like that, of course, and we should probably always surrender to its power as a form of catharsis, but we need to be prepared to bleed, as Joni Mitchell once sang.

Interestingly, when I think back to the process of turning these rare operas into a twenty-five-year strand our audiences would grow loyal to, I recall an element of sniffiness about them within the business. In opera, one can spend an entire lifetime engaged in discussion about quality, validity, seriousness, authenticity or the cynicism of a composer. I have, for example, a particular and mischievous fancy for delivering critical treatises on the deficits in Mozart operas to conductors, because it usually generates frothy rage. Complexity is a quality scholars appreciate, but the operas I favour are often simplistic in plot, and the music is thoroughly manipulative. I don't think I have ever heard someone use the Italian origins of these operas as an attack strategy, because, whilst it may have taken time, many Italian composers eventually reached the higher echelons of approval, and Italian opera is greatly respected in general. In academic terms, the discipline of musicology was created by Germans (*Musikwissenschaft*), and so, up until fairly recently, Italian opera wasn't studied or given academic parlour room to the same degree as Wagner or Mozart. Even Puccini, by now possibly the most popular opera composer in history, was given a bit of a cold shoulder.

In the early days I felt as though some critics and commentators, along with certain sections of the audience, were unable to acknowledge that raw stories were, to me, what being Italian was all about. These composers had found a way, through their music, to characterise suffering and pain; and some of the scenarios they created were actually not a million miles away from bits of my family history: my great uncle Michele really did have to bolt to America in the early 1920s because he'd shot someone over illicit love. These works are an emotionally unrestricted, all-out assault on the psyche, and there was a narrative afoot that declared such stuff as vulgar. Some of it is – but I didn't care, because I and my family history have a vulgarity in part.

It is fair to say that the view of all this has changed somewhat, and there is a growing acceptance that Puccini's breathtakingly clever curation of an audience's response took no less genius than the more elegant achievements of Verdi. In the final analysis, if I want to give someone their first experience of opera's potential impact, it is one of these operas – say *L'amore dei tre* by Italo Montemezzi, which ends with three corpses on stage – I would put them in front of.

* * *

At home as a child, opera wasn't regularly heard, although my uncle Matteo was often found spinning a Mario Lanza compilation. I'd experienced it at school through the choir, and in the early 1980s I started to attend the odd performance on tour (usually to impress a potential girlfriend and to amplify my Italianness).

What I did hear a great deal of was traditional Neapolitan music by singers and composers such as Roberto Murolo, Sergio Bruni, Renato Carosone and Mario Merola. Neapolitan song has been around for centuries, and one of its most famous staple songs, '*Te voglio bene assaje*' ('I Love You Very Much'), was once accredited to Donizetti. Modern examples of Neapolitan song from the 1950s onwards vary enormously in instrumental style and arrangement; Murolo and his solo acoustic guitar are my favourite version – the voice and the lyricism of the words and music are genuinely mesmerising. The songs are, of course, entirely about love and heartache (except for a couple of novelty ones about drunk donkeys). My mum's favourite was '*Voce 'e notte*' ('Voice in the Night'), which is about unrequited yearning for illicit love. The music Mum played on her stereogram via a collection of seven-inch vinyls drawn from tattered paper sleeves was a constant accompaniment, and she would sing along, often getting a little tearful. It was nostalgia and the sense of loss of her marriage, I think. She had a nice voice and, of course, could sing the words authentically. I don't wish to insult modern opera singers who perform some of the more famous *canzone Nnapulitan*, but I have yet to hear one – even from Italian singers – who can come remotely close to the authentic dialectic inflections required.

Much like late-Italian operatic repertoire, these songs represent the place from which they emerge, in a literal, spectacularly authentic way, and the memories they evoke are frequently overwhelming. When Mum was ravaged by dementia and couldn't even open her eyes, let alone communicate, I was encouraged by a project Opera Holland Park ran with the charity Playlist for Life, putting a pair of headphones on her and playing her favourite songs through them. In no time at all her lips started moving, her eyes flickered and from her mouth emanated the words and music she was listening to. It may well have been that her entire life had come close to being completely erased from her memory at that point, but '*Voce 'e notte*' remained, and it is one of the most lovely and beguiling songs you will ever hear.

It had taken Mum at least ten years to accept that my job in opera was legitimate. I had certainly never engaged in conversations about Mozart or Verdi with her, because that would have made her even more suspicious. At first she didn't understand the job I was doing, suspected it was hogwash and that I would probably be better off working in a more secure job at 'Macadonol' (McDonald's). A social worker she could understand, a painter and decorator – a bin man, perhaps. Lou, having been a District Line train driver for years (she used to brag about that), went on to work for a large international telephony company. He had been building computers since he was a teenager and was very good at it. Mum knew he worked in 'compudas' and seemed satisfied with that, because it was Lou and he was sensible. I think she probably just suspected me of being a bit of a charlatan and a 'beeg'ed'. We were never a family who praised each other – and that's still pretty much the case. I don't think my brothers have ever congratulated me for anything – the way we express this seems to be through taking the piss. I think there is an acknowledgement somewhere in there, but it has certainly made me very efficient when it comes to self-appraisal.

Eventually, though, when I had sustained my position at Opera Holland Park for a few years (something Mum had been sceptical I would achieve), she began to come to see operas, and enjoyed the attention everybody would give her. She'd look at me working a room or meeting people, or perhaps giving instructions to staff, and, when I returned to her, she would give me her signature sideways stare and call me a 'flasha wenka'. Then she'd criticise the Italian emanating from the singers – which is a bit rich given how bloody awful her own version of Italian was.

She continued to have an annual presence at Lasagne Night, when I cooked a very opulent version she had taught me (beef shin, egg, salami, fresh mozzarella). The company would be fed once the show had gone up, and they would gorge on 'Lidia's Lasagne'. I think Opera Holland Park still have the recipe on their website.

Even though she was never quite sure of what it was I did, its scope or importance, as far as she could tell, it was paid work and they hadn't fired me. She remained a cynic, and always suspected that I was just trying to draw attention to myself – it just wasn't proper work. If she saw that a newspaper, radio or TV station had interviewed me, she was most likely to treat it with disdain and consider it braggadocio. I do think she was eventually proud of what I became; although I cannot remember a single time when she actually said the words, I am certain she was.

Not long before she died from dementia, Opera Holland Park brought a group of singers to the care home she was in for Carols at Christmas. I sat next to Mum's crumpled, seemingly vegetative form as they performed. Several of the team, who'd grown fond of Mum and her ways, were emotionally distraught at the sight of what had befallen her, and for obvious reasons I tried hard not to show my own feelings. I failed. They sang for a roomful of residents, but I know really they sang just for Mum, and I'll be for ever grateful.

Everybody has regret for the things their deceased parents missed. For me the pain comes from her not seeing her grandchildren's journey into adulthood. For several years before her death she was really not here at all. My work at Opera Holland Park brought recognition in the form of an OBE and, given Mum's great interest in the royal family, I would have liked to have taken her to Windsor Castle for the investiture. She had strong views on the members of the Family – who she approved of, who she didn't – and everything was a conspiracy. She certainly believed Diana was bumped off, but she liked 'Principessa Anne', and it was she who pinned the medal on me. Because I am a vocal lefty, I got quite a lot of stick for accepting that medal, but the simple truth is that I was accepting it on behalf of my mother, and I know she would have been beside herself.

Right through my teenage years and early twenties, I was really only developing like anybody else might. I was instinctively blagging my way through my life and career and was trying to recoup (or rescue) with the chances given to me by my education, and I was furiously catching up – but I needed tools and believed any form of exoticism would help, although I was a bit too highly strung.

I like to watch the BBC TV programme *The Repair Shop*, in which a group of craftspeople mend and restore family heirlooms in a barn. People bring in objects and describe what they mean to them – 'This was my grandfather's alarm clock' – or it could be an artefact, something mundane like a small transistor radio, or a glittering historical keepsake that reminds them of their father, mother or uncle. The owner of the item describes childhood memories and relationships with relatives and how the object represents a life together. As a piece of television it is remarkable, veering from gentle nostalgia to absolutely gut-wrenching displays of grief, all wrapped up in what at first appears to be feel-good teatime telly. I can be rendered dripping and distraught by it. Watching these people become emotional about such things makes me realise just how little of that I have had in my life. I had no relationship to speak of with either set of grandparents – not in any enduring way, where they loom large and positively in a person's life. We had a fractured family and a father of no consequence. There are youthful memories of big gatherings, but when you are that young you don't understand, you just *feel*. When you grow and begin to grasp the nature of conflict, separation, despair, the feeling of loss only sharpens.

Mum was the only real 'ever-present' I had. The family in Montecorvino was the closest I came to an adoring, expressive network of relatives, and they were a long way away. I'm not surprised I put them and my heritage on a pedestal, because their existence and my connection to them framed everything. Today my brothers and I have decent relationships, we all have our emotional restrictions and we have been known to fall out, but since one is in the Highlands of Scotland and the other is living in the USA, our interactions are largely digital these days. We also have a half-brother – the product of my father's relationship with the woman he left my mother for. I only met him when my father died, even though we knew of our respective existences for decades.

I have children making their way in the world, and a wife, so I am content and not alone. In my head, though, I think I have been solitary for a long time. Some readers will know what this contradiction means in real terms. I have become so adept at covering my tracks, as it were, that this paragraph might come as something of a surprise to many who know me, but suddenly feeling a desperate need to escape a room full of people remains a common occurrence today. Insularity and a desire for solitude isn't really the first thing people associate me with, but it is a driving force in my life. It was when I was a child, too, and I am starting to believe that my behaviour and truculence as a youth was because the real world kept interrupting my inner one, making demands of me.

That inner world was where I immersed myself in music, mainly, but when I was at Woolverstone drama was the answer, too. In a play I was able to be someone else, and it is not irrelevant to this conversation that during the rehearsal process of a play I was an exemplary student, whereas at most others I was an insufferable shit. In fact, I was a different person entirely, and playing someone else gave me new methods with which to interact with the world around me. So as an adult, perhaps my attachment to 'performance' as an Italian keeps me afloat mentally? I *am* a forceful arguer, and tend to fight fire with fire, being especially suspicious of those who wish to impose their will with *ipse dixit*s and to claim superiority because they do it with more measure and softness than I do. In this realm I have taken much from my mother's unwillingness to countenance such insidiousness: 'Fuggoff!'

The question I am asking myself in this book is whether my Italian family background has created that person who *needs* a costume. Would I still feel out of place and solitary if I were to have grown up in Montecorvino, rather than in London? Would my psychological template be just the same were I not to have experienced this geographical and cultural dissonance? Our life as children was certainly emotionally dynamic, as much a direct consequence of our Italian world as it was of our poverty. Experiences form you, of course, and there are hundreds of small, sharply defined events that still circulate in my psyche. I remember things every day and see them again in my mind's eye; and although I am fairly used to facing them, and even analysing them, the idea that they haven't shaped me psychologically is a nonsense.

In a recent conversation with my eldest daughter, after watching a documentary by the journalist Fergal Keane, I realised that I very likely have PTSD from the experience of my brother's death. That event, and images from it, are still figuratively in the front of my mind every day, and any mention of it can snap me a little more every time. There was a particularly brutal period of several years that started with divorce from my first wife, included a serious injury, Matt's death, my mother's spiralling dementia and my father's death and ended with the loss of Mum. Whatever was 'wrong' with me before that period began, my resilience was tested to the limit during it, and I have undoubtedly emerged more sensitive and prone to depressive episodes, and the desire for the balm of seclusion – where I don't have to speak or listen to anybody – has grown.

When I began to contemplate writing about all of this, I had the idea of asking other British-born Italians about their feelings and experiences. Surely there are thousands who think like me and feel as disconnected as I do? I'd originally hoped this book would be a dispassionate examination of the issue, with data and interviews, and I did consult quite a few 'Britalians', mainly by way of a questionnaire. There are some remarkable similarities between their answers, most of which mirror my own experience. Unfortunately, because I am not an academic, and as you have seen, I get easily diverted by melodrama, the sociologically scientific version of the book has fallen by the wayside. I decided that if I were to report their stories at all, there would be a responsibility to tell more of them. Suffice to say that most of those I spoke to reported many of the fundamental feelings of dislocation I experienced, but some also took a very different view of their identity. One of those who hasn't grown any attachments to Italy in the way I have is my eldest brother, Lou. Below are his answers to the questionnaire.

***

Obviously you were aware of your Italian heritage, but how did it generally make you feel? Did you feel unusual?

As a kid in Woodstock Grove, yes. Lots of taunting from other kids, to the extent I hated my name and persuaded Mum to give you an English name when you were born. Can't say I FELT different, just hated BEING different, with all the attention this brought.

What are your significant memories of this Italian heritage/lifestyle?

Parties for religious events – baptisms, communion, etc.

Did you play up your background or did you keep it quiet?

Never played it up as a kid, but then I never tried to draw attention to myself anyway. Got even more stick at secondary school. As an adult, no, but it was hardly a secret either.

Were you proud of it?

Not as a kid – it brought too much unwanted attention. As an adult no real feelings either way – hard to feel proud of an accident of birth.

Has that view changed or altered as you got older?

No.

How did your background affect your life, if at all?

Apart from denying it as above, can't think of anything.

Do you think your family background has affected your outlook, personality, behaviour?

Yes, but was that because of the dynamic of dysfunction or was the dysfunction caused by the nationality? Were Italian men more handy with their fists than English men? I believe we are born with certain personality traits, but upbringing plays a part. I was determined not to be like Dad in terms of neanderthal attitudes and violence.

Do you consider yourself Italian or British?

Neither – ENGLISH!! Not Italian, because I was not born or raised there. I can't believe anyone BORN in the UK feels British as there is NO British identity, rather English, Scottish, etc. There is no notion of 'the union', the UK is made up of separate countries. Only immigrants to the UK feel 'British'.

What do you like best about being of Italian heritage?

Nothing springs to mind…

What do you like least?

The arrogance of Italian men – something I have always been conscious of from childhood and actively tried not to be.

What are your best memories of living among an Italian extended family?

Get-togethers, meals, etc.

What are your worst memories of it?

Nastiness, long-held grudges, arguments.

Anything else you want to say/add?

Yes, you are a knob.

* * *

I don't know what to say.

My brother grew up in the same household as I did, and had the same influences, but because of certain family dynamics (he was much more aware of the process that led to my father's departure than any of us), the picture of Italy that formed in his young mind was a malign one, based essentially on having encountered arrogant, violent men. It nevertheless illustrates that identity can be a conscious decision – or, more specifically, the rejection of an identity can be, or the refusal to succumb to instinct alone. Knowing this, it would be easy to devalue my own sense of where I come from, but I continue to insist that I just feel the way I feel, and he would do the same. Although he is not in the least well disposed towards the English establishment he does feel an *affinity* with England – it is worth noting that Lou has lived in Scotland for many years and is a fervent believer in Scottish independence. Somewhere along the way he has reconsidered his cultural attachments, which is not to say he wears a kilt every day, but it's a hint that national identities are not entirely unimportant to him.

The immigrant experience is not as well documented in the UK as it is in, say, the USA. Books exist that tell the stories of individuals whose families originate in the Caribbean or the Indian subcontinent, and, as former colonies, these countries have a very particular relationship with the UK, for obvious reasons. But Italians and other Europeans have really only begun to articulate their feelings since Brexit ruined everything and truly othered us. Despite talking about the racial abuse I have received, I am acutely aware that it has been nothing compared to that experienced by others. Everybody, from whatever culture, believes their own heritage to have a distinct character, and I make no claims for Italy beyond the reality of its contribution to the UK and its place in the national consciousness. My obsession is how my relationship to Italy has provided the curtilage for my life.

Feeling attached to a distinct cultural heritage, be that a nationality or a religion, is often soothing, a balm for inner turmoil, but that connection can also be to profound *historical* pain; pain that one might not have directly suffered but which nevertheless resonates through the years, like a ripple in a pond. One could point to several groups of people in the UK whose personal identities are acutely informed by historical events. There are others, but the Jewish and Caribbean communities have in recent years come to the forefront of public discourse and exemplify the sort of historical pain I am talking about – one that contemporary communities find a deep connection to; the first primarily (but not only) because of the grotesque savagery of the Holocaust, and the latter as a consequence of slavery as well as more recent events such as the Windrush scandal. It is alarming to note that there are people who wish to keep these events as a part of the distant past, who say we ought to move beyond them, and are irritated by reference to them.

It is important to acknowledge that my story features nothing as dreadful as genocide or slavery; but what happens to our forebears is still relevant to who we are and how we feel. For me, it is the poverty and misery I know my mother experienced as a young woman, the family dysfunction and how Italy was beset by war and chaos, which almost took her life. These things are as informative as the unique loveliness of so much of where she was from, and which I detail herein. But brutal injustice, even that suffered decades or centuries ago, can cut through the consciousness of descendants.

For example, while I cannot speak for the journalist Danny Finkelstein, I suspect his powerful and highly praised book (*Hitler, Stalin, Mum and Dad*) about his family's experience of the Holocaust is likely to have reinforced his perception of how that history shapes him and his identity today. By way of a fictional juxtaposition – but no less potent a demonstration of the concept – Shalom Auslander's satirical and subversive novel *Hope: A Tragedy* tells the tale of a Jewish New Yorker finding an ancient and irascible Anne Frank in his loft. Quite apart from the monumental consequences of such a discovery, the principal character's mother is forever referring dramatically to how she suffered in the Holocaust, even though she was born after the war. Not one of the family, however, feels the need or desire to take her to task over that historical reality; they just understand. It seems that even a writer as renegade as Auslander insists, amid the humour and caricature, that the reader also understands this connecting thread within the identity of his characters.

BREXIT

The presence of racial abuse in all the stories of those I consulted in my survey could explain a lot about this sense of disconnect and 'not belonging' that many of us seem to feel in the UK. I don't actually believe it is the driving force – it is a by-product. Critically, however, post-Brexit, the experience will be very familiar to many who are immigrants from a European (or any other) country or who have heritage there.

A billion words have been written about Brexit, the most unfathomable act of self-harm a country has carried out since Mussolini's Italy decided to throw its lot in with Hitler in the Second World War. Whatever Brexit was and is (as we speak it is an evolving disaster that some continue to present as an opportunity), at its core it was a destructive act: everything it is predicated upon – despite the supposedly sensible, if chimeric, technical arguments some might posit in its favour – is divisive. Its champions, feeling the weight of its failure, insult and rage against the population on social media and do everything they can to stir up anger among the dwindling band of hardcore Brexiters. Every now and again, a nugget of 'good news', such as trade deals with inconsequential benefits, struck with countries on the other side of the world, are given the full propagandist parade in friendly media. On the other hand, these same people believe it is imperative, driven as many of them are by disruptive far-right ideology, to keep people suspicious of government, to keep them from facing reality. It is their view that the destruction caused by Brexit, not to mention the robbing of so many rights and privileges, is in fact *not* the 'proper Brexit' they wanted. All rules and safety regulations have to go, for example; and every major issue or event is presented as a trick or a conspiracy – the most prominent example of this being the COVID-19 pandemic: it appears from circumstantial evidence that the majority of vehement Brexiters are also dedicated anti-vaccine activists.

In the context of this book I want to talk about how Brexit changed how I saw both England (for it is a peculiarly English thing) and thence myself.

An expression established itself in common language soon after the referendum in 2016: 'Not all Brexiters are racists, but all racists are Brexiters.' It wasn't just the exceptionalism of Brexit or the way in which a paring knife was knowingly worked into the cracks of society and used to prise them open, to release a pent-up insecurity that inevitably found its target on foreigners; it was that I realised how a great many people in Britain suddenly decided that they were *better* than me – or the nation I identified with – along with many other nations the UK had vanishingly little to teach about cultural society or a way of life. Brexit was a touchstone for those who had always despised immigration of any kind. Reasonable people who came to support the idea of leaving the European Union were lied to on a monumental scale, and the course of Brexit has created a culture in which the government, filled with people brought to power by the vandalism of it, is brazen about lying to the public's face without a flicker of shame or guilt. It has been truly catastrophic for the contentment of the United Kingdom and will, I fear, only get worse from here. Influenced by mainly American fascists, our political system is being polluted to a quite grotesque degree.

Perhaps the greatest shock has been the way in which those who fetishised the concept of Brexit were prepared to trash the few core things the UK had always seemed to me to do well:

fair play, democracy, integrity, due process and the rule of law, a sense of community and equality. Of course, this stance wasn't adopted by the majority of people, but it was the philosophy that eventually won the argument and propelled politicians of a disgusting hue into parliament, and it has driven toxic, brazenly corrupt and chaotic governments ever since. The economic and social nightmare of Brexit is now evident to all but the fundamentalists, but the real harms will last a great deal longer than any economic turmoil. Socially, the country is now damaged beyond repair, it would seem, and since the current opposition party has decided on an 'all votes, any votes, any cost' policy, they are now required to maintain the fantasy of a functional post-Brexit society and economy.

The original referendum vote in 2016, and the events that have followed, precipitated a desire in me to grasp harder at my European roots, but they also convinced me that I was justified in my fifty-year-long discomfort. I can hear the howls of protest as I write, but I'd like to think I'm not talking about at least half of the country. Brexit, I am afraid to say, forced me to ask myself the question, 'Why am I still here?' Indeed, since 2016, countless Brexiters have asked me the very same question. Having got their Brexit, and encouraged by politicians in government, they have now moved on to increasingly violent, hateful language, but now it is aimed at immigrants and asylum seekers, and is moving inexorably, under the rallying cry against the 'woke', towards a plethora of minorities. The stench is unmistakable.

The England my mother came to was very much traumatised by the experience of the war. Mentally and physically scarred (even I played on bomb sites), England needed and invited foreigners, but never really welcomed them. Italy also had scars – deeper ones, in fact, since Italy is where what is generally believed to be the most punishing invasion of the final Allied push to end the war happened. The destruction and death was total in some places, and Mum carried those events with her. Oddly, I don't think she held anything against the English for their suspicion of her in the early years – why wouldn't they have a problem with the arrival of those considered enemies not too long before? She was coming from a place of thorough-going poverty, disease and strife (even though Italy's recovery would move at a greater pace than that of the UK), so even her slum home in west London and her insecure work were an improvement. She valued enormously the way in which England gave you a fair crack of the whip and supported you with a social benefits net. She didn't resent wealth, and, having been a domestic when she first arrived, had a sort of subservience to her employers' status, while refusing to accept any abuse. In short, she quickly learned to understand the social hierarchy in England. For many, many years, she was the housekeeper (a second job, of course) for the High Court judge Sir David Croom-Johnson and his wife, and there developed a mutual adoration between her and their family.

I recall many conversations she had with other Italians who might display a form of cultural one-upmanship; she recognised the things that made Italy distinctive, but she could be scathing about its attitude to looking after people. Over time, she became fervently opposed to the Conservative party because she perceived them as being at war with the poor. Thatcher she despised ('a fucky evil beetch'). Fundamentally, though, Mum thought the English were decent, and said it was an honest country, operating on fair play and integrity. In later years, when my own political beliefs had formed, she and I would argue about that final point. I have always considered the British political system to have a corruption at its core, but Mum argued fervently that the Italians were the masters of corruption, and didn't agree that any such thing occurred here. What she didn't realise, I told her, was that in Italy the corruption was in the open and the British were just more subtle about it, but to her mind the NHS, the justice system, democracy, the social security net and so on trumped all of that.

Mum didn't see Brexit, so I will never know how her opinions might have changed or whether she would have seen things differently. She may well have felt compelled to return to her home country, as so many Europeans have, suddenly aware that they are no longer welcome here.

After the referendum result, hate crimes against foreigners grew enormously. As if to demonstrate the basis upon which many had voted, hate crimes against Muslims and people of colour grew most of all. It was evident that Brexit had offered itself up to xenophobes as a way of getting rid of all the foreigners in our midst, not just the Europeans. I'm not interested in the squeals of those who object to this characterisation, by the way – it is clear what drove an enormous number of people to vote for Brexit, and many always knew this dark underbelly existed in the UK. Now, the people who would once have been seen at the head of small demonstrations of fascists and racists are at the heart of government. It has been a long project of insurgency and lies.

Indeed, Brexit did drive EU foreigners away, and that is now having a negative impact on our public services and economy, but in the process we have come to see what really motivates those architects of Brexit. Their obsessions now include the people escaping the wars we have encouraged, and their repulsive language and policies towards them, driven by the rage of impotence, is plain for all to see. In a deeply ironic twist, non-EU immigration to the UK has sky-rocketed as the country seeks to fill the gaps.

The most painful and alarming illustration of how the post-referendum period appeared to set free the bogeyman of racism was the Grenfell disaster in 2017. Seventy-two people, including my friend Debbie Lamprell, died in the nightmarish fire that swept through a tower block in west London. Very quickly afterwards, a narrative that those who'd died were all illegal immigrants was established. This was entirely false – not one of those who died was an illegal resident, but many of the people on the death-roll *were* north African and Muslim. Conspiracy theories proliferated – some suggested the flat in which the fire began was a bomb factory – and although all were completely disproven by the entire body of evidence, this mattered little to the people who saw Grenfell as a symbol of 'open borders'. 'It is terrible what happened, but if they weren't here illegally they would be alive' was a common utterance on social media, and, almost seven years after the disaster, I continue to see similar language on Twitter (X).

The true point is, of course, that even if every single one of the dead had been illegally in the UK, why would that affect the scale of the horror or the empathy we should feel in response to it? It was chilling to see the dismissal of all that death based on the grotesque qualification of immigration status. The Grenfell disaster's role as a touchstone for the demise of a nation's compassion – or at least its conditionality – was only surpassed by responses to the pandemic, in which tens of thousands of deaths among the elderly were shrugged off with the assurance that they would have died of something soon anyway.

Grenfell truly alerted me to the fact that sections of the UK population have been radicalised and have a long way back to their humanity. Would this attitude have prevailed without Brexit stirring up the issue of immigration? I might be making a false conflation here: perhaps many people would always have thought in these terms (not exactly something to be proud of in any case), but I am almost certain they wouldn't have felt as free to voice these notions so assertively.

I don't have black skin or speak with a foreign accent, but there are some who appear to recognise Mediterranean traits in my face. Brexit and the prevailing government narrative have enabled these people to feel comfortable expressing their bigotry. Fairly recently, a man on a bus decided I was clearly out of place. He had been aggressive and needlessly rude to a young Asian woman and her small child, and I'd taken issue with him for it. My firmness with him had made him simmer in his seat until he couldn't help himself and began to mumble racist epithets aimed at the woman, but also at me. I took issue again, and he snapped back with, 'Where are YOU from? This is my country!'

I was a bit taken aback, especially since I'd adopted full-on Fulham-speak when I'd remonstrated with him.

'I'm from here, mate, Fulham,' I replied.

'Yeah, course you are,' he scoffed.

I had said enough to him to demonstrate that I was indeed a 'local', but his foreigner radar told him I didn't belong and had no right to prevent him from expressing his feelings to a woman who was equally unwelcome in his world. I might have been born and brought up here, but where I was *really* from is what mattered to him.

It matters to me, too, but he was the walking, frothing embodiment of the reason I think I am writing this book. I recently saw a thread on Twitter (X) in which a British Bangladeshi under the name @shihabJoi mentioned how he'd been irritated by being asked what his cultural origins were. The person who'd asked him had done so in a benign sense, and the tweeter acknowledged this, but he was still irritated because he just wanted to be considered a Brit, not a Bangladeshi, even though he admits he often talks about his culture. I felt compelled to point out that no matter what he feels, there are some who will never consider him a Brit, regardless of where he was born or what passport he holds. Conversely, as I said at the start of the book, it appears that some, who say I should consider myself British having been born here, are often the same people who think the colour of somebody's skin is a disqualifying criterion.

My identity is something I value, so why shouldn't the English? They do, and, indeed, should. But I'd argue the angry English have come to overvalue some of the wrong things about their culture, and seem to eschew the aspects that actually made the country what it is (was). And central to the problem is the sense that accepting and valuing other cultures somehow threatens

English identity and thus reveals an insecurity. Consequently, in the noise and fury, it seems to go unnoticed that foreigners tend to value the tenets of traditional English society more than those who hate them for somehow polluting it.

I really do have a pride in the things Italy does well – not just the obvious things, the stereotypes of cars, food, fashion. The idea that one might be *proud* of a country is a little odd in any case, especially if it is exclusionary or suggests any form of supremacy. I certainly don't feel that way. Perhaps what I mean is that I take satisfaction? Have admiration? I find it in small things, traditions that despite the modern age will endure in the form they have always had. I even felt it when watching a concert by the band Genesis, recorded at the Circus Maximus in Rome with 500,000 people in attendance. The lead singer, Phil Collins, turned his microphone to the crowd at a particular point in 'I Know What I Like', and the audience sang the melody together in a way I can only imagine an Italian crowd doing it. Even I am aware that it sounds ridiculous, but it really seems to mean something. I suppose it is what happens when, as the dandyish angel, visiting earth from a monochrome heaven in Powell and Pressburger's *A Matter of Life and Death* says, 'One is starved of Technicolor up there.' Powell and Pressburger are also a reminder of another aspect of British history: its arts and creativity. Through the brilliance of their film-making, they demonstrated a defiance as well as extraordinary innovation, and the greatest living American film director, Martin Scorsese, is an unbridled devotee of their work. As 'English' as their work was (Pressburger was Hungarian), they always had an international outlook.

In recent years, the cultural life of the UK has been under constant attack, and at time of writing, our Brexit-induced government, through cuts to budgets as well an explicit denigration in the curriculum, is degrading the importance and presence of the arts in British life. This book is not meant to be a comparison between the things Italy and the UK do well, but the process of writing it has drawn attention to the attack on things Britain has always been famous for, and that applies to the cultural, political and societal fabric of the nation. This process of activated decay has accelerated recently, but it has been unfolding for a few decades at least.

Several years ago I recall being invited to an urgent gathering of arts leaders at the Globe theatre, to formulate a response to the arts-exclusionary EBacc curriculum being proposed by the government. This piece of educational policy, in its white paper, actually labelled arts subjects of 'no value' and sought to promote more technical subjects above all else. As I sat in the meeting, looking at the Globe, I reflected on the excruciating disgrace that we should be having such a conversation in the country of Shakespeare and countless other monumental cultural icons. Indeed, the Globe was the result of an American director's passion for creating it, and he did so without the help of government for many years. The aforementioned film, *A Matter of Life and Death*, includes a heavenly trial and a scene in which Roger Livesey's character is forced to defend England against the criticisms of an American prosecutor. The prosecutor plays a radio commentary of a cricket match by way of ridicule.

'For England,' says Livesey's character, in response, 'I'm ready to call John Donne, Dryden, Pope, Wordsworth and Coleridge, Shelley and Keats.'

Well, quite.

The greater part of the British public *do* have a suspicion of the creative arts – particularly my bit of it, opera – but that isn't likely to change much with the continued lack of arts education (or even just exposure to the arts) in schools. The exception to that is that private schools do value the arts, and so our audiences, for the classical arts in particular, will continue to come mainly from certain sections of society. I fear there is another book to be written on this topic, but I mention it because it has been a painful, inexorable course that one can track all the way back to Thatcher, who believed that anybody who likes culture should probably have to pay for it in full themselves. Our recent governments take not so much a financial approach to it – although they do slash budgets – but a dogmatic one, in which the greatest threat from cultural society is knowledge, free-thinking human sensitivity and 'leftist' ideology. A chilling familiarity is evident (or should be) in that last sentence.

The result of this long decline is that for tens of millions of people born in this historic bastion of great art and music, there exists a void where theatres are never visited, opera is encountered only in the form of eager amateurs on TV talent shows and any expression of humanity through performance is considered 'woke' and/or elitist. It is unimaginable that I would experience in London what I did in Milan a few years ago, when, between leaving the airport and arriving at my hotel, three ordinary citizens (including a taxi driver) had excitedly told me that Verdi's *Attila* was opening at La Scala that evening. While Italy can claim so much in the realm of mankind's cultural enlightenment, Britain has a spectacular history of its own that it appears not to value at a core population level, which seems to suit this government perfectly. The greatest tragedy of Brexit – and it *is* a tragedy – is the way in which it has radicalised a large section of the English population into being ignorant, wilfully or otherwise, of the very things that *should* make them proud of their country.

People like me do not 'hate' Britain, even though we may feel emotionally or culturally disconnected from it. Feeling out of place for so long has always, in my mind, been 'my fault', my problem, and it wasn't because people actively tried to make me feel that way (beyond a few). I could at any time have chosen to identify more with being English – as many people of Italian and other ethnic descent have. I have absolutely no issue with those who make that choice, but I know how that man on the bus would treat those who'd made it. Personally speaking, my most profound discomfort today is with the emergence of people who wish to isolate and effectively dumb down the country, make it look insecure and distant from everybody else while wrapping themselves in patriotism and now an overt toxic nationalism. The truth is that many British people are horrified at how the country is self-harming, and it should come as no surprise that many find more to relate to on the continent across the Channel from which we are now cut adrift. British people have had their right of movement, to live or work in Europe, completely removed from them by a minority. And that really is a savage curtailment of rights.

Since Brexit, my own discomforts and emotional connections have transformed from an internal quandary to a full-blown consideration of whether I want to be here at all. The structure of this animosity reaches to the top of government, and is in part enshrined in new legislation. I am told that I should wait it out, that it will change one day, but I have concluded that it is now hardwired for at least a generation.

We all knew what Brexit represented – we knew that it was really a Trojan horse for something worse, built by people who find regulation, law, democracy and decency to be a bar to their ambitions – mostly in the realm of disaster capitalism.

A vox pop with a young woman, filmed the morning after the referendum in 2016, was recently reposted to Twitter (X), and it is very painful to watch. She was asked how she felt by a TV reporter and, with growing upset said, 'I feel like hate won. I feel like we are watching the stirrings of fascism in Europe again, and I genuinely never thought it would be *my* country that did that. I never thought it would be *us* who would run to the right and turn our backs on the world. I thought it would be America, that America were the people who were so filled with hate. Not us.'

Her eloquent, grief-stricken words summed up exactly how millions were feeling on that morning.

Practical issues are the greatest barrier to my moving elsewhere – one child still at school and others making their lives here, for example. My older children are in the process of acquiring the

Italian passports to which they are entitled, and they also feel a strong sense of their Italian heritage. Their mother is Scottish, and Brexit has also made that country's independence more desirable to many there, so my children may end up having two ways to turn. What has surprised me is that my two eldest, in particular, have very powerful memories of the Italian part of their family: their Nonna, of visits to Montecorvino. But most startling of all, to me at least, was learning that they saw me and my brothers as an integral part of the Italian picture.

The wedding of Zia Ines. My Nonno Perillo is on the left and Nonna Anna is next to him.

Mum.

Mum (left) and a friend on the passeggiata, *Montecorvino, circa 1950.*

Nonna Volpe and three of her children. My father is on the right.

Mum in the park with all four of her children.

Me, Matt and Lou on the train to Italy, 1974.

In the garden at Woodstock Grove. Me, left, with only one shoe.

Matt and me on the ferry to France, on the way to Italy, 1974.

Nonna Anna.

Zio Rolando.

Matt in Montecorvino, during the time he was sent there to live and escape his miscreant life in London.

My father and Nonno Volpe, at Woodstock Grove, prior to my birth.

MONTECORVINO

If life at home was a hybrid of Italian music, the BBC and The Beatles (my mum loved 'I Want to Hold Your Hand'), a little oasis of Italy in west London, it was in Montecorvino, on holiday, that this continuing assumption of identity would find its real source material. Our family enclave in London was connected by an invisible thread to one across the mainland of Europe and into the Mediterranean. In my young mind Montecorvino might as well have been a city with towers of gold.

When you're a kid, extremes have a big, lasting impact. Montecorvino Rovella and our journey to it offered lots of them: arduous travel, heat, sensational landscapes, long lunches, dozens of relatives, florid language, poverty, deceit, jealousy, hysteria. But there wasn't much glamour – certainly not in the traditional sense – because it was an altogether earthy place.

When we travelled to Italy, it was by train. From Victoria to Dover, then a ferry, another train to Paris and then by bus across Paris from the Gare du Nord to the Gare de Lyon, the terminus that sent trains south. In the waiting room, packed with sleeping travellers and characters of all kinds, we would wait for several hours for the connection to Rome. Once, a man in a gendarme uniform held court – much to the chagrin of the rest of us, who were trying to sleep – and, through a cloud of Gitanes smoke, regaled a pair of French students with stories of goodness knows what, for goodness knows how long, until even he eventually laid his head on a rolled-up coat and went to sleep. The slumbering bodies were packed in on the floor, side by side like sardines, and if you wanted to leave the room to visit the toilets you had to gently pick your way through them, finding little gaps into which you could, teetering on one foot, place the other.

My eldest brother Lou had decided to make the first attempt at the journey, with, inexplicably, his heavy metal camera in his hand, a Russian Zenith that could have been made from granite. As he gingerly stepped across the bodies, the camera fell from his grasp and clunked the gently snoring gendarme on the forehead. Had the camera not been in its leather case, the result could have been bloody, but it was merely shocking and left a V-shaped dent above his substantial nose. Fortunately, Lou had kept hold of the strap, which unravelled to the full extent, and in the blink of an eye, as a gymnast whips her ribbon, he had retrieved the camera and danced like Baryshnikov over the remaining sleepers and out of the door. So swift was he that the gendarme had not the slightest idea what had happened to him as he awoke in agony, to look around bleary eyed and confused at a silent, motionless room. I had seen what had happened and was sniggering quietly into the crook of my arm. Lou, who was shy and easily embarrassed, refused to return to the waiting room and stayed outside until morning.

From Paris, the train to Rome was the epic portion of the journey, during which we slept in a compartment with four couchette beds. The train took us through the Alps, through the Mont Blanc tunnel and into Italy and to Rome, from where another train to Salerno and then a bus to Montecorvino Rovella completed the journey. All this over twenty-four hours, with several suitcases and four children. Mum was a saint. The journey itself was always something of an adventure, and I loved to stand in the choked gangways outside the compartments, feeling the breeze of the open window and watching the Italians chatting animatedly and smoking. Passing through the Alps at night remains among the most evocative memories I have.

Montecorvino sits at the edge of a national park in the Picentini Mountains, close to Battipaglia, where, it is reasonably and fairly claimed, the world's finest buffalo mozzarella is made. The town was established as Mons Corvinus circa 89 BC, after the people in the area – Picentes from the Adriatic coast who had been sent there as a colony after the Romans defeated them – rebelled again, got another kicking and were then forced into more easily controllable villages. The Romans built a castle there, known as Nebulano Castle, the ruins of which can still be seen, and the place has been occupied by Longobards, Normans, Angevins and Aragonese. It is also known as the 'City of Astronomy' by dint of the fact there is an observatory at the top of a local mountain. There is a famous legend: that of the Somnambulist – a woman who lived in the Nebulano Castle and was thought to wander the town murdering people – but it turned out that sleepwalking with a knife in her hand was cover for some illicit nooky she was pursuing. The most spectacular historical fact about Montecorvino, however, is that it is the place where events thought to have inspired Shakespeare's *Romeo and Juliet* occurred.

In the fourteenth century, there were two powerful families in Montecorvino – the Damolidei and the D'Arminios – who didn't like each other much. In the town was an oak tree at which people were executed, and this was popular entertainment for the entire town. Davide D'Arminio and the Damolidei beauty, Maria Teresa, clocked each other at one of these occasions, and it was love at first sight. Secret love, family outrage, feuds, captures and imprisonments followed, but it ended quite well when a priest intervened and everybody relented. However, it is thought that the story inspired the novella by Masuccio Salernitano that, in turn, gave the cue to Shakespeare, who is thought to have read it. The link sounds plausible, and was the subject of serious historical study a couple of decades ago, the conclusion being that it may well have inspired the Bard's play. The best part of this story is that my grandfather's house is on

Vico Damolidei, a short, hooded walkway that passes beneath the centuries-old house purported to be the Damolidei home, and which includes the crossway balcony of legend.

I can't claim I knew all this back in the 1970s. To me, Montecorvino was an impossibly exciting and almost outlandish small town on the side of a mountain that offered lots of adventure and family fun. On my first memorable holiday there the mountains above and around Montecorvino were ablaze with grass and forest fires, with conflagrations popping up all over the place. There was no apparent alarm from the locals – it just seemed to be the way of things at the height of the blistering summer. It was the potency of the heat I was at first stunned by, the one element that controlled and dictated the experience. Cicadas chirruping all day, the weight of a Mediterranean sun on our heads, the light – this was another world, all right, and it was one I couldn't quite believe had nurtured my mother. It was such a historic, dramatic landscape, and its recent history of war and terror, along with its more ancient one of Greeks and Romans, was mysterious, profoundly exciting and impossibly important. So a small Italian mother of common stock, who'd grown up through some of this history and played as a child among the ruins of Paestum, had about her, even for me, a kind of glamour and experience it was difficult to comprehend. A movie of my era, loved by all of us in the playground, was *Jason and the Argonauts,* and a major scene was filmed at Paestum, so it even had Hollywood glitter. I made sure everybody knew that, because I had also played around the temples of Paestum, I too was dusted with some of that glitter.

Mum knew strange things about vegetables she ate as a child, and would explain how she'd grown up eating plants we all now perceive as weeds. When I was at school in Suffolk I'd always loved seeing the swallows over the cricket field, and on one visit Mum exclaimed, 'Oh, *rondine!*' Just knowing what these birds were (and having her own word for them) made me think she was cool, and I recall feeling very proud of her.

Rolando, Mum's mushroom-collecting ex-trapeze-artist brother, was usually our host for the stay. I am not entirely sure why, because his was a small ramshackle stone house in Nuvola, an ancient and decrepit district on the edge of town, and he had just two rooms. The bedroom was large, however, and around a central double bed there were several other camp beds squeezed in. Matt and Lou might go and stay with Mum's other brother, Mario, who had a larger house, and on some nights we would all stay with him too. But Rolando was my favourite uncle, and I enjoyed staying there, even though I had to share beds with my cousins in a room that might eventually sleep eight of us. In the morning, his wife Anna would wake us with a small cup of lukewarm espresso that I would swig, then rest my head back on the pillow.

Waking up to an already ferociously hot morning was exciting. My cousins Lidia and Ferruccio would drag me into the lanes and rocky hills to trap lizards. Our languages were different, but I had smatterings of Italian, and would continue to learn the language throughout the stay, as children do so much more easily than adults. It would be dialect, rough and florid, but we played together happily, understanding each other perfectly well. I became part of their gang – a curiosity, no doubt, but they were fiercely protective and possessive. Passing an old man who was calmly killing his chickens at a table outside of his front door, Ferruccio suggested to him that I should have a go. The old man tried to give me a short lesson on chicken slaughter, how I should hook two fingers either side of its head and lever it backwards until the neck snapped. I got the levering bit right, but not the force required, and ended up yanking fruitlessly at the chicken's head. The old man took the bird from me and tore its head clean off, but the real horror occurred when he chucked it to the floor and it ran around aimlessly, to a backing track of my screams.

Detaching parts of animal anatomies was a theme. We spent a lot of time trying to catch lizards, and I committed the rookie error of grabbing a rather large one by its tail, which it promptly detached from its body, leaving the limb wriggling in my hand, and ran up the stone wall of a bridge to hide in a nook in the brickwork. Recovered from the nightmarish trauma of the tail, with screams subsided, I took a large branch and began to poke around in the hole a few feet above me. Having had enough of this, the raggedy-arsed reptile leaped from the hole towards me and landed on my head, and Nuvola once more heard my shrieks.

Of course, during those early journeys to Italy, I wasn't aware of the dazzling contrasts between the north and south, and it would be years before trips to Milan, Florence, Turin, the Lakes and Rome in particular gave me an understanding of the different faces of the country and the people. Montecorvino, though, would become the Italy I knew and the one I would take home to school.

At Spineta beach, directly west of Montecorvino at the edge of the plain above which the mountains towered, we'd go to the messy, rubbish-strewn stretch of public sand and look longingly at the fenced-off private section, whose fees paid for it to be cleaned and raked to spotless beauty every morning. Occasionally, at the crack of dawn, our entire family would fill a convoy of cars and spend the day at Spineta, a multi-generational party of my uncles and aunts, my cousins and their children. There is something special about early mornings in the southern Mediterranean, the stillness, warmth and light, and to this day I am profoundly addicted to them, waking early on holidays to experience them. After a morning playing in the surf, at or around midday, along with the hordes of other families, we would retreat to the cool of the pine forest backing the beach and set up plastic fold-up tables and chairs, on to which were piled kilos of panini, home-made wine and watermelon.

There was no culture among Italians of staying at the beach all day; it was a few hours in the morning, a picnic lunch and then home for the afternoon snooze. The public beach had basic changing facilities, but they were some way from the forest, and so, while hiding behind a tree to change into denim shorts for the journey home, I one day caught the tip of my willy in the zip, and the screams – yep, again – brought half the forest to my aid, led by my traumatised mother. This legion of onlookers also included my female cousins as well as everybody else in the family. While Mum was consoled and calmed, the older members of the family each took a turn in trying to free me from the predicament, and, inevitably, arguments broke out. One of my cousins told his brother to go fuck his mother, while his mother, who was there at the time, was busily tugging at the offending zip, succeeding only in adding an extra couple of teeth to the entrapment.

It was always this way with us, minor issues that descended into pandemonium, small vignettes of southern Italian angst. It still happens today, and I am prone to do it with my children too. Italian hysteria born of excessive concern is contagious, and every time I look at two fingers on my right hand I'm reminded of this fact.

* * *

FINGERS AND FURY ON THE ROAD TO EBOLI

Mum's determination was boundless. She'd find the house Vito lived in if it was the last thing she would ever do. Houses with blackened stone may all look alike to some, but to Mum, a Campanian, they were as different as fingerprints, and she just had to remember the shape of the windows and the fall of the sun as it set. And when she found it, Vito would know we wanted to travel to Eboli, where Mum's idolised aunt Francesca lived, as old as the hills now, and who didn't know we would be coming. We would just hope she was at home when we arrived.

That's how we always did it – there was no phone call, just an arrival in a street or lane, hot and dusty, cicadas chirruping. Often we didn't know the door, or the house, and then Mum would shout out the name of her cousin, her friend, her aunt. And from a window a head would emerge, often one that didn't belong to the person we were looking for, to tell us that Giovanni/Tina/Ovidio has moved to Battipaglia/Acerno/the north. Or our luck would be in, and we'd be told that, three doors down, the target could be found. They would tell us to wait while they came down to show us where to go, and Mum would thank them, not in the least embarrassed to have disturbed the day of this unknown neighbour of whoever it was we sought. But this neighbour was nosey – they all were – and wanted to know who this stranger and her children were, and what better way to find out than facilitate a reunion?

The neighbour would begin digging straight away, asking if Mum was related to Giovanni, etc., and she would reply that she was his cousin/friend whom she hadn't seen for years. But the neighbour is only just getting started, because next comes the question about family names, and Mum always answered by saying her maiden name and then adding that she had married Francesco Volpe, '*figlio di* Luigi Volpe, *da* Sant' Eustach', Montecorvino.' It was like a script that she trotted out, every time.

'Ah, Luigi Volpe, *un uomo buono.*'

I never liked that. Everybody said my grandfather was a good man, but I know he took Dad's side. He came to London and never came to see us, because Dad was his first-born and he couldn't betray him. How did seeing the grandchildren of his first-born become a question of loyalty? How is he a good man for having such a skewed view of the world? Mum never argued with whoever said it, though, despite finding it as laughable and ironic as I did. She had every reason to fire a fusillade of pent-up bitterness and anger at the neighbour, but she was more interested in finding her cousin/friend. Now wasn't the time. I wonder if every episode like this took a small chunk out of her, again and again?

Vito, for whom we had been searching for some time, was an old friend of Mum's who worked as a taxi driver. He would take us to Eboli, where we would search the streets, vaguely in the right area – but it had been a long time since Mum last saw her aunt. The streets, narrow and dark, would have to be reconstructed in her mind from memory. The day was hot and would only get hotter. I didn't want to go to Eboli – I didn't know this aunt for whom Mum had a religious affection. I would have to sit in a living room, shrouded in blinds and curtains to keep out the heat, while Mum drank coffee and spoke to a very old woman who she'd say used to be the most beautiful woman in Eboli. I wanted to go to the beach.

Why didn't they have phones in Montecorvino? We trudged the streets in the heat, eyes from every corner and doorway on us because Mum looked different, with her coloured blouses bought from the North End Road market and her highlighted hair. People from Mum's past greeted her, but I could see their suspicious eyes scanning her up and down. She wasn't one of them any longer – but jealousy would drag less in their chests if they knew what she ended up with.

When Vito's head poked from the window to answer the shrieking of his name, it was bald. His eyes were tired, so I reckoned he had been sleeping, and he didn't seem pleased.

'*Chi é?*'

'*Sono* Lidia!'

From the way his eyes lit up in recognition, I could tell he had a soft spot for Mum. Violins were playing. Mum had told me he used to work with her in the tobacco fields before she came to England. I think *he* had other ideas for them, but Dad got there first. I couldn't help wondering if Vito would have been a better father.

With Mum shouting up to Vito, soon the whole street discovered we wanted to go to Eboli. He told us to wait – twice. He emphasised the second '*aspett*'' as though he thought Mum might run off with someone else again while he trotted down the stairs. Vito had a kind face. He looked at Mum like a man who shared a youth with her. I didn't know what they were saying exactly, because they spoke too fast for me to catch it all. Mum explained that she wanted to go to Eboli, and Vito was clearly saying he would take her, but it would have to be tomorrow. Great, so that's two days' beach time wasted on this. They were arranging a time for the next day, then started to reminisce and remember other friends, and Vito's hand rested on Mum's arm. Then he looked at me and asked my name and age, and Mum told him I was her 'baby' (the last-born) – I always hated it when she said that.

'What a beautiful boy. He looks like you, Lidia.'

But I don't look like *you*, do I, Vito? I thought.

When, the next morning, we stood at the side of the Second World War field gun that sits in the small main square of Montecorvino, an ornamental reminder of the destruction of the past, I prayed Vito would forget his promise – Eboli felt no more appealing than it did the day before – and when he arrived my heart sank. He had a small green van with windows, and when he got out to open the door for us, he could look down on the roof. And he wasn't alone: there were two people already in this little bus. Worse: Vito says he has more to pick up. This was going to be a bad journey – it was only eight in the morning and already the heat was crushing. I knew Mum just wanted to show me off to her aunt, but I wished I was at the beach.

Vito ushered us to the side door and tilted the rear seats forward, revealing a makeshift bench on which Mum and I could sit. But there was a large box on the other half of it, so I had to sit on her lap.

'Mum, I don't want to sit on your lap!'

'Shuddup,' she said, glaring at me.

The door slammed shut.

I looked at the people in the van. A woman with a hairnet sat in the front seat next to Vito, her fat shoulder brushing against his arm as he changed gear, and she was talking at breakneck speed to Vito, as though just resuming the conversation they had been having when they'd stopped to collect us. Actually, she was talking *at* Vito. I could see his eyes in the rear-view mirror, and he looked back at me and winked. He never looked at Hairnet, even when answering her. Hairnet turned to look at Mum, smiled and said, *'Buongiorno.'* Mum, peering around me, returned the greeting.

'She doesn't stop talking,' I whispered to Mum.

'Shuddup,' Mum said through gritted teeth.

'They don't understand me anyway, and I am whispering.'

'Shuddup!' she growled. 'If you show me up, I fucky killa you.'

Why *does* nobody in this town speak English? I thought. There was a single one, as far as I could tell – a woman who married a local man when he lived in London and came back to live on a small lane down in Sant' Eustach'. Beyond that – nothing. English was an entirely alien language.

The other passenger was a young man, thin, wearing a checked shirt with a large collar, who never looked at anybody and was reading a folded newspaper on his lap. He was sitting on the row of three tiny seats in front of our bench, so I guessed we'd be picking up two more passengers for those seats. The van was struggling up the mountain roads already, so I worried what would happen if we filled it with even more weight as we stopped again, by a stone fountain in a village I didn't know, and Vito leaped out to open the door for an old man in a flat cap and baggy trousers. How did these people manage to tell Vito they wanted to make a journey somewhere? Did they shout up at his window, too?

'Ciao, Vito,' he said, as Vito opened the door for him. The door slammed shut and the van rang from the shock, the air pressure changing. Flat Cap slid the little side window open and lit a cigar, and he greeted Hairnet as though he knew her well. Checked Shirt just glanced up and nodded. As Vito revved the engine to get the reluctant van moving again, Flat Cap half-turned, as though he had a stiff neck, to look at Mum and me,

and I stared at the cigar hanging from his mouth. He was trying to work out who Mum is. Hairnet was laughing at something she said, Vito gave me another wink, Flat Cap nodded at Mum and ignored me. Everybody looked at Mum in the same way, sometimes recognising her and talking, remining each other of who they were related to, and then inviting us to lunch – long lunches – with people we didn't know. It is hard to refuse such an invitation in Montecorvino. People take offence very easily.

It was so hot in that van, and it didn't seem to have suspension. As Campania crawled by the window, I was wishing I was on the beach with my brothers, where the day before we had been surrounded by jellyfish on the three-tiered wooden raft we had hired. For an hour we splatted the jellyfish with the raft's oars. I wanted to see if they were back today.

Vito called back to Mum that she should come and visit him and his wife for lunch one day. Hairnet looked sideways at him suspiciously, and Flat Cap blew a cloud of blue smoke up into the roof.

'*Si, certo,*' replied Mum.

Great, another long bloody lunch with someone I don't know, I thought. I was just glad Flat Cap didn't recognise Mum, because I didn't want to have lunch at his house.

This journey was taking longer than I thought, but there was still one more to pick up, and the heat was withering, so I opened the small triangular window that levered out just far enough for me to hang my arm into the breeze. We stopped at a small row of shops in a larger village I had never heard of – it just appeared at the bottom of a mountain road. Vito couldn't seem to see the person he was collecting and we waited, but eventually, after some discussion with Hairnet, who looked disdainful, Vito released the handbrake and begins to pull away.

'O! Vito! Vito!' The voice was shrill and panicked.

Vito slams on his brakes and looked in his wing mirror. The side door in front of us opened, and a young woman carrying a shopping bag leaped in, panting, as Flat Cap shuffled quickly to the middle seat. Shopping Bag babbled that she thought she had missed him, that she was sorry she had kept him waiting. She was adjusting her feet, finding a space on the floor to squeeze her shopping bag into. The door was still open, and I found a space in its frame to grip.

And then the door slammed shut.

The violent forward contraction of Shopping Bag's head into the back of Hairnet's seat was not because the tip of Flat Cap's cigar had showered her with hot embers, it was because of the scream that had made him convulse and jerk his hands into the roof of the van. The scream was still at its full pitch and volume as Checked Shirt was exclaiming, '*Che cazz'?!*' – his first words of the journey. Mum's face was pressed hard into my back because I had gone straight and rigid.

'Whaddapen!? Whaddapen?!' Mum bellowed from the side of her mouth.

Vito turned back towards us with a look of alarm and was asking the same. Shopping Bag was still recoiling, utterly bewildered at the sound that had erupted as she slammed the door shut. She hadn't even noticed we were behind her.

My fingers were trapped in the door, and I had begun to worry that they had been severed. I didn't want to lose my fingers – not even the tops of two fingers.

'The door!'

'*La porta!*' screamed Mum.

'The fucking door!' I screamed louder.

'*La* fucky *porta! Mannaggia!*'

Mum was beginning to panic too, because she didn't like to hear her children scream unless she was giving them a good hiding – she knew what was causing it in those instances. Otherwise, she hated even to hear us cry.

Vito leaped from his seat and came to the door, a look of concern on his face that would have passed muster at a funeral.

'Don't open the door! My fingers will fall off!'

But he opened it anyway, and my fingers didn't fall off. Everybody slid quickly out of the van, and Vito tipped the seat forward so I could get out, grabbing my wrist to help me.

'Don't fucking touch me!'

Mum gave me a shove, propelling me into Vito, who kept repeating, '*Calma, calma.*'

Nobody was calm, however. Not Mum, for sure, who was traumatised. Vito told her it was OK, my fingers were not on the floor, but Mum screamed some abuse at Shopping Bag, and Vito gently remonstrated with her, saying she shouldn't blame Shopping Bag.

Strangely, having feared that blood would be spurting everywhere, I was surprised to see my fingers were not bleeding at all, but two open slices adorned the top knuckles of my index and middle finger. I could see the whiteness of the bone, like two angry little smiles. Hairnet had come to the side of the van and was chanting '*Mamma mia*' to herself.

'*Acqua!*' shouted Flat Cap, and Shopping Bag took a bottle of water from her bag and began to pour it on to my fingers. More screams.

'No!' shrieked Mum.

Shopping Bag shrugged her shoulders and said something in response, but Mum told her to go and fuck her mother. I always liked this, and I almost laughed, but Vito seemed undone by it all and could only stand there watching, with a hand on his forehead and the other on his waist. Hairnet was still just saying '*Mamma mia*', and then everybody began to argue about what to do while I cried. Vito looked close to doing the same. Poor Vito – you *would* have made a decent dad, I reckon.

'Fuckinella, I godda 'eadache now,' complained Mum.

Checked Shirt hadn't said or done much while they all fought over the best course of action. I expect he was used to it at home; perhaps this was how his family behaved, verbally abusing each other over the amount of salt in the pasta. He didn't seem the type to tell anybody to go and copulate with their mother, even over something important. As the fury and confusion grew at the side of a road in a village I didn't know, Checked Shirt ushered me into the pharmacy we happened to have stopped beside as we waited for Shopping Bag. It was only when the pharmacist was halfway through dribbling iodine into the cuts that anybody noticed we'd gone, and by the time she had strapped the fingers together with gauze and a strip of plaster, Vito's passengers were all standing around us, watching, murmuring their approval. Checked Shirt had left and was sitting in the van. Vito placed a consoling arm on my shoulder and helped me climb back into the van and on to Mum's lap again. He looked at me in the rear-view mirror a few times more with concern.

'Mum, was Vito ever your boyfriend?'

'Fuggoff.'

* * *

Many years later (perhaps as many as twenty), on another visit to Montecorvino, Vito was still working, and we used him one afternoon, although I didn't recognise him or the van. He looked quizzically at me and, without speaking, took my hands in his, found the scars on my two fingers, smiled, and said, '*Mi ricordo*.' Then he did an impersonation of me screaming.

I relate these stories not to illustrate that these people were inherently hysterical (they were), but because they cared a great deal about me and my brothers. We were a precious asset to them, their 'English' cousins. Southern Italy is also extremely child-focused, and you haven't seen spoiled kids until you have been there, so when one of us, usually me, got into a scrape, even the people I didn't know would leap into protective action. I think I was fifteen years old when, riding a scooter along the main street of Montecorvino, I drove into the back of the car in front, tipping the bike and me sideways on to the pavement. Several men sitting outside a bar leaped from their seats, dragged the driver out of the car and remonstrated with him. It had been entirely my fault, but the driver still came sheepishly around to the back of the car to apologise and help me pick up the bike. His unquestioning contrition did make me wonder if the fellas who'd taken him to task had a certain reputation.

Mum had four siblings, three brothers and a sister. Isidoro was the oldest, then came Mum, then Rolando, Mario and finally Ines, who had bolted north to Florence after her marriage. Isidoro, whom my mum always seemed suspicious of to some degree, had seven children at the last count, Rolando had four and Mario kept the numbers low, with three. Ines had two sons living with her in Florence. So I had a lot of cousins, some of whom were adults by the time I first met them. It was generally the case that each had to be visited regularly for lunch (dinner wasn't a big thing), but, because it had the largest dining space, Isidoro's house was the one we often ended up at, behind a small front door in a narrow stone alleyway that led off the main square of Montecorvino. The heat of the afternoon was reduced a little by the darkness of the street, but in the living room, dominated by a huge dining table, with sofas lining the walls, it was hard to catch a breath sometimes.

We ate like kings, even given the family's relative lack of wealth, and the women and girls would ferret around the attached kitchen preparing the feast once they'd returned from working in the fields. Isidoro's wife knew that pasta fagioli – rich with heavily cooked beans, nuggets of pork cheek, slabs of gelatinous fat, parmesan rind and dissolved tomatoes – was my favourite, and made it often; even as a starter, it was brought to the table in a vast bowl. That was only the beginning – unctuous meat, cooked for hours in a tomato sauce, salads and a variety of vegetables and breads would follow. Everything was topped off by pastries and a watermelon so large it was bought home in a wheelbarrow.

The lunches were long, loud and frequently argumentative – well, always, actually – and Pasquale, the third-eldest son, would join us with his wife and small daughter. He was brash and comical and liked to learn English swear words, which I taught him avidly, and he'd then embroider them into a lavish monologue in Nnapulitan, reducing Mum to fits of laughter. He was easy to like. Lucio, the baker, was less demonstrative, the spitting image of his father, but he still had to compete for loudness when required. He had opened the bakery – a hard life, for sure – and back then lived in a farmhouse owned by his wife's family a little way out of town. When we visited him, peaches, oranges and figs would be plucked from the trees in his garden. Mario, Isidoro's third son, was small, wiry and quiet. Giovanni, the youngest brother, was serious and opinionated and liked to argue. There was another sister, Anna Maria, who was severely disabled after childhood vaccinations, and died at the age of seventeen.

Mum adored all the daughters of her siblings, probably because she had always wanted one of her own. Isidoro's daughters were Antonella, Clementina and Rita, who were sweet, wise for their age and affectionate; they took Serge and me to the shops with them to show us off. The shop at which we were most frequently paraded was the pasticceria, where a collection of cakes and pastries for the post-lunch dessert were acquired. Cannoli, zeppoli, castagnole and, the king of them all, sfogliatelle (layers of wafer-thin, crisp, burnished pastry, arranged in a clam shape and filled with deliciously sweet, lemon-tinged ricotta cream), were arranged in beautiful paper on a tray. Food shops in Italy – butchers especially – have a gorgeous way of wrapping their goods.

In the evenings, it was all about the *passeggiata* on the main thoroughfare of Montecorvino, via Cappucin'. Hundreds of people would parade noisily up and down the street, talking to friends, arguing, with children constantly buzzing around, screaming and crying. Young teenage courtships would begin here, feuds would simmer or even resolve, and my brothers and I were the visible curiosities. My cousins would link arms with us, walking three or four abreast, and greet their friends, introducing us to each with great excitement. It was sometimes difficult being the subject of the collective gaze, but I loved the event, the small stalls of street food, pizza, gelato and granita served old-style, with ice scraped fiercely from a large block. My favourite was *musa di porco*, which is pig's snout boiled, cut into chunks and served with lemon and salt.

The *passeggiata* is undoubtedly theatrical, but it is about socialising. I couldn't think of anything similar at home that fostered such a feeling of community, of posturing and posing. Mum and her brothers might meet at a café while we youngsters paraded ourselves, and there, too, they would argue and gesticulate over coffee, pastries, maybe a pizza and granita to ward off the stifling heat of the early evening. I loved seeing them together and would always eventually work my way back to them so I could sit and listen to them perform.

Mum seemed to have a very prickly relationship with Isidoro; she never really seemed to trust him and thought him selfish, too. He wasn't as open and friendly as my other uncles and seemed to worry constantly or was up to some scheme or other. He walked around the house in a white vest, rubbing his abdomen and complaining of pain. If Isidoro took any of his family to task, Mum would leap in and defend them, and at times like that it was very difficult to follow the conversation because it would speed up three-fold, involve several voices and descend into bog-dialect that can sound almost Martian. Usually, Mum was jumping in on the side of Isidoro's wife or any of his daughters, and by the end of the conflict, at least two could be crying and one had stormed out of the house.

These almighty dust-ups were magnificent; I loved them, mainly because they even happened when nobody was particularly upset about anything and could erupt in an instant. It just seemed to be the dramatic and dynamic way in which people there communicated, and the bits we couldn't understand Mum would explain, mid-row. If she wasn't screaming and gesticulating at Isidoro (who in response would sit quietly, with a confused look on his face, as though he had no idea what he had done wrong), she would be rocking with laughter.

Watching Mum with her older brother was fascinating and educational, too. I knew enough by then about the Italian family home: the women did everything – cook, clean, wash the clothes – and they never spoke out of turn. Isidoro was very much of this mould, but Mum was clearly not paid up to the idea; she called a spade a spade – or, in his case, a *stronz'* a *stronz'* – and Isidoro was taken to the cleaners in front of his family more often than he would have been used to. I never thought they liked each other much, yet they would often seem close. But the arguments could be brutal and would often end suddenly, in a stream of profanities, like the big final flourish of a fireworks display, after which peace would return.

Isidoro: *Fa fancul' a chi ta muort'* (Go fuck your dead relatives).
Mum: *Fa fancul' a mamat'* (Go fuck your mother).
Isidoro: *A te e sorot* (And your sister).
Mum: *A te e freid* (And your brother).
Isidoro: *Zucame 'e ppalle* (Suck my balls).

Thinking back to my time in Montecorvino, it isn't difficult to understand why my experience of the place and my family formed the basis for my emerging identity. My memories are visceral – the smells, the sense of an extreme climate, the architecture. The language was a powerful element, too, because the lyrical and unique way in which my family spoke was an other-worldly dynamic that engaged me totally. Everything seemed to be a performance, and nobody, whether it be a pair of old men outside a café, a bus driver or women hanging washing from balconies, spoke in a measured or quiet way. It was always dazzlingly animated, full of dramatic inflection and is a method of communication that has undoubtedly remained with me to a significant degree.

It is odd how memory works, the pictures it retains from thousands of others that vanish into history. The notion that my mother was from this place, had a past and a childhood in it, was something that always bewitched me, but it was often just the way in which she seemed to *belong*, to behave as the people there did, and instinctively knew what to do and say. She would change from the woman I knew in London – she was at home. The rituals we followed seemed to remain most powerfully in my memory, the simple, mundane things that nevertheless told a story about Mum's life and demonstrated that this was the place that created her.

A simple example would be the nightly walk home from central Rovella to Rolando's house in Nuvola. It wasn't far, perhaps a mile, but we always did it in the dark, it was always a hot evening, the cicadas would be loud (a sound I still find comforting) and there were long, steep hills to negotiate. Usually we were accompanied by a couple of relatives who would see us home, and they would be speaking animatedly with Mum for the whole walk. What always struck me was how she seemed unfazed by the steep hills – her legs were always strong and defined in the calf, and in my childhood mind I made the connection between this physical attribute and her ability to stroll a hill without apparent discomfort; she must have spent her life walking the steep mountain roads. My brothers and I would be forging ahead, looking for rats and chucking stones into the darkness; but although Mum wasn't lagging behind as a consequence of physical challenge, she *was* stopping every thirty yards to engage more fully in the conversation. Standing still for a moment and gesticulating seemed necessary in order to make a point more powerfully.

'Come on, Mum! Why do you have to keep stopping?'

'Fuggoff!'

When we eventually reached the narrow, dark streets of Nuvola, the conversation didn't abate – nor would the volume. Even though it was late and shutters were open on dark rooms, nobody ever poked their heads out to quieten the women or us children. There were still many in-use pig sties beneath the houses, and so the organic smell of the animal pens and the quiet snorts of the pigs provided the atmosphere. The sties were unlit, and we'd peer over their half-doors to look at the animals, but could rarely make out anything more than an outline. It was quite forbidding at the time.

This simple walk home every night was a strange, almost dangerous melange of cicadas, rats, arguments, the smell of swine shit and the sound of snuffles and oinks. But every bit of it taught me something, immersed me in an experience I'd never have had in London. And there were many vignettes like this, rituals that never just passed by the inquisitive child that I was – all of them became imprinted in my memory.

Each day in Montecorvino, then, was a new discovery, even if it was no more than a walk home, a trip to the beach or a visit to a relative, because each of them represented my mother's life, a story she might tell, a rich cultural event that even I knew was unique to the life of a boy from my side of the tracks in Fulham. It was all romantic in one way, shape or form, experiences framed by old, pitted and powdery buildings, spectacular countryside and an extraordinarily dynamic way of life that swung from beauty to monstrosity, forever retaining an edge of danger or a link to a disturbing past. Children and young people romanticise things and I most certainly valued a melodrama.

Spending time there was never boring. I remember feeling very much part of the community when I went about the town or the surrounding roads and villages. I wasn't especially sensitive to the fact that people often stared at me, and we were known as something of a curiosity; I always considered I was being welcomed home, even as a child. It was also a place of unbridled freedom compared to London, because in Montecorvino I could borrow a cousin's scooter and ride it beyond the horizon if I so wished. I did it from the age of around eleven years old and, because I rode bicycles in London, I had no fear of Campanian country roads. Chugging up and down the mountain to Pugliano or down towards Macchia and the coast, I rarely, if ever, had a destination in mind; I was just wandering, experiencing the climate and the countryside, unsupervised, unhindered and unafraid – mostly. At home I would always be wary of boys from other estates as I walked around the streets, and I would often get into pointless fights; but in Montecorvino, although I frequently encountered small gangs of local kids, they never showed hostility. Curiosity was the primary motivation for any attention they gave me, and sometimes I'd stop and talk to them in broken Italian. Some even knew who I was, because back in the 1970s that part of Italy did not have much foreign tourism at all, so everybody noticed a stranger.

Every day of riding the roads was an escapade, and I often found myself in places I didn't know, or on roads that seemed remote, surrounded on either side by huge, towering reeds or crops. The smells and sounds, coupled with the heat and light, are overpowering in my memory, as is the trepidation I would frequently suffer as a consequence of being lost.

I would always, however, be cautious of the remote level-crossing on the road to Spineta beach, because Mum had told me of how, when she worked in the tobacco fields, their work's bus had once broken down between the barriers, which had then lowered. The bus, full of inevitably screaming workers, was trapped on the tracks, and all the men had leaped from it to push the bus out of the way of the train hurtling towards them. They made it, but the story had stuck in my head. I simply didn't trust the barriers, and I would look several times, both ways, gingerly inching out until I was certain, and then accelerated to the other side. To this day I mistrust level-crossings.

Those weeks of wandering deepened my immersion in what I only really ever saw as my Italian idyll of scorched grass verges, pungent wild herbs, pine forests and cicadas. It wasn't all perfect, of course, because the poverty was on show in most places I went, and my family had moments of upset and drama I wasn't always entertained by. Summer in Montecorvino was a vivacious montage of all these things that, collectively, helped form my developing personality and sense of self, but also left me confused when I returned to London. Montecorvino wasn't *home*, exactly, but neither was it a holiday destination.

Whatever Montecorvino represented to me, it was, and remains, the place that characterises the fractures in my family, with both my father and mother's families being there. Fair to say that the Volpe side had rather more members in London than in Italy, with nearly all of my father's siblings eventually coming to the UK. Nevertheless, each visit to Montecorvino carried with it the potential for further rupture, drama or upset, and our time was spent mainly with my mother's family. There was one obvious figure who loomed large in our consciousness, who cast a shadow over our trips, and that was Luigi Volpe, my grandfather.

* * *

The fulcrum around which my developing identity turned was naturally my mother. It is hard to articulate the contrast between her Italian life and the one she eventually led in London, but for me, given that my father had fled when I was six months old, her achievements as the sole guardian of us four boys, tiptoeing through the precarious poverty of late 1960s and early 1970s London, were nothing short of miraculous.

It is important to acknowledge that broken families, grudges, extreme dilemmas and intensely dramatic (and often tactical) reconciliations are an Italian cultural reality. When I think of my own psychological frailties, it occurs to me that most of them are shaped by the consequences of this almost casually pursued operational model. Insecurity, inability to trust, cussedness, pride, anger, rejection, secrecy: all of it emerges from a lifetime of disruption, fear, violence (both real and threatened), dishonesty and the cumulative effects thereof. In essence, being Italian can be damaging to your health. Those things people appreciate and understand about Italians, the cultural stereotypes, as it were, are really just the consequence of centuries-old ways of doing things, the side-effects of our accumulated experience.

Mum's devotion was all-consuming, but it was edged with a flinty determination that saw her take whatever steps might be necessary to keep us alive. I think there were few limits to what she was capable of doing to protect us. By the time I was just a toddler, the family had split along loyalty lines.

Luigi Volpe, my Nonno on my father's side, somewhat respected and publicly known in Montecorvino, was faced with a choice: take the side of his son, who had behaved pretty abominably, or continue to support and respect his daughter-in-law and grandchildren, who'd been at the receiving end. For a while, he tried to service both sides and we would sometimes stay with Nonno and Nonna when we went to Montecorvino. Our relationship with him was episodic, and in later years, whenever we were in Montecorvino, the prospect of going to see him felt precarious and unpredictable.

In Naples, there is a saying: *Quanno te miette ncopp' a ddoje selle, primma o poje vaje c' 'o culo nterra* (When you try to ride two saddles, sooner or later you'll end up with your arse on the ground). And so it would come to pass, although it was our arses on the floor.

Nonno would quite often visit the UK, because before long almost all his children had emigrated here, with his daughters settling mainly in Somerset and his two sons in London. All had growing families, and his eldest – my father – was the apple of his eye. There were pictures of Nonno in our Woodstock Grove home, all before I was born, but at some point, on an important anniversary, when he visited and gathered everybody in the UK to celebrate the occasion, my mother and her children were suddenly excluded, and no party invitation came. We were outside of the family pack. Zio Matteo, driven by his overt and almost obsessive principles, decided that his father's behaviour was a betrayal, and from then on was almost entirely estranged from him and my father for a long period. He was ever-present in our lives, and we spent a lot of time with our cousins and Zio Matteo, who, despite being angry and hard to cope with, was a surrogate father.

I'm really not sure why my grandfather took the course of action he did. Maybe it was just too awkward for him to take a neutral position, or maybe he didn't give much of a fig. I do know he eventually came to justify it to himself when he wrote a book of his life and mentioned how we had become disrespectful of him. That justification was on account of something I did. The event itself was a perfect illustration of the performative way in which Italian families go about their dramas, and, with hindsight, it was almost comical, but its effects lasted for a long while.

CAUSING A SCENE

I was in Italy with Mum at around the age of eighteen or
nineteen, and she had suggested that we go down to visit Nonno
Volpe, in Sant' Eustach', in the lower part of Montecorvino,
where he lived. Mum had never once in her life sought to
prevent us from seeing either our father or any of his family, and
we would visit Nonno or other members of the Volpe clan. We
knew exactly where Nonno would be: either standing, leaned
against a rail next to the church, or sitting under a tree in the
tiny piazza, around which a stone bench was constructed. He
was always at one of these places, but if he wasn't we would
knock on the door of his ancient home, which we used to stay in
as small children.

The road down to Sant' Eustach' is a long, straight hill and
at the bottom sits the inevitable church. From a fair distance
away we could see Nonno standing at the rail to the side of the
church, a piece of street furniture I have always thought must
have been installed solely for him to lean on. Because I hadn't
seen him for some years I was surprisingly excited to be doing
so, but even his casual stance was emphatic, his expression one
of deep thought. He eventually turned his head to focus on the
people approaching in his peripheral vision, and his lazy gaze
sharpened when he saw us. 'Nonno!' I said, and held my arms
out wide for a hug, but when I got to a few feet of him, he turned
180 degrees, silently, and stood with his back to me, diverting
any such greeting. At first I was confused and stopped in my

tracks, thinking perhaps that he hadn't actually recognised me – I'd become an adult since I last saw him. I know he would have heard we were in town, so I was sure he expected a visit.

'Nonno?'

No reply.

'Nonno, *sono io*, Michele,' I said, still thinking that recognition was the issue.

He remained silent and with his back to me. I was close enough to touch him.

Mum, who'd been ten yards behind me as I quickened my excited step, caught up and realised at once what was going on. 'Come on, *andiamo*.'

'Nonno?' I said once more. He didn't move or speak.

He was turning his back on me in a very real and demonstrative way, but he was probably doing it as much to my mother.

***

At this point I should report on an event seven years after this moment. When I married my first wife, Alison, we went again to Montecorvino for a few days before a holiday in Sorrento. A message had been sent to my mother that Nonno and Nonna wanted to see us at the Ferragosto, when everybody gathered in the square for music and food and fireworks. They tried to persuade her – twenty-six years after he'd last deserted her – to reconcile with my father, who was unhappy with the woman he'd left her for. Not a word was spoken about the shuddering halt to which Nonno had brought our relationship a few years earlier. It was as if it had never happened.

***

Back in 1984, his atrocious behaviour had hit me hard and set me aflame. Mum told me to forget about it, that he wasn't worth it. Readers may have experienced such a brutal, flagrant rejection and therefore understand the emotional chain reaction it ignites, but it is difficult to articulate. Ostracism takes many forms: by omission, by distant behaviours, by neglect, by fierce letter, by email or by text. But at a distance of a few feet, ostracism by body language gives you no time to react except to be mute, perplexed and a little desperate. This is especially so when the person doing the ostracising is someone who should never be reasonably found doing so. It wasn't long before I had processed the event in the only way my psychological makeup allowed, which was to arrive at a boiling fury, my hackles raised and my strong sense of respect and probity outraged; that was often how I responded to things that wounded me emotionally. I also clearly recall thinking that I had a new appreciation for how my mother must have felt many times, over many years. I was embarrassed, too – by the age of eighteen I had become exquisitely sensitive to how I appeared in front of others – and my mind turned to what can only be described as revenge.

Later that evening, I walked back to the piazza, where I knew my grandfather would be, under the tree that he and his friends would frequent. I walked slowly and deliberately past him and sat at a table outside of the little spartan bar a few metres from the tree, ignoring him. This obviously caught the attention of everybody there – they knew who I was – but they hadn't seen what he had done earlier in the day – and I could sense the murmuring, the whispering and that all eyes were on me. Being the subject of collective southern Italian ire and glaring attention is probably what it feels like to be stalked by wolves as they slowly close the ring around you. And there is no nuance, everything is, and would be, black and white. Nonno was staring at me too because he was being embarrassed in front of his friends. I suppose he thought we had left by now, gone elsewhere, and that nobody would ever realise what he'd done. One wonders what he expected to happen once he realised I was there: did he think his behaviour would be easily brushed away? That I would approach him as though nothing had happened so he could keep up appearances? How dare he, I thought. Nonno was a respected and well-known individual in Montecorvino, and now his grandson was showing him no respect at all. His friends, I could see, were quietly asking Nonno what was going on, but, beyond a few shrugs, I have no idea what he said to them. His passivity in all this seemed to give them the impression that he was lacerated, helpless and innocent. They soon became angry about it, and one by one they began to gather around me.

As ever, a small familial dispute was turning into something a good deal bigger, and it was also providing entertainment for the village. Layers of history were being revived, and, excitingly, rumour might just about to be confirmed, the Inglese were in town and it was payback time for someone, and so forth. I was creating a story, some historical moment that would be passed down in future and, although I haven't checked, by now the story of Luigi Volpe's grandson could well involve a shoot-out. The reality was significantly less dramatic, but it was a fact that both the menace and the gathered throng were growing.

'What are you doing? Why are you not speaking to your grandfather? He is very upset.'

'Have you asked him what happened earlier?'

I repeated this to everybody who approached me. I recall glancing around and seeing a young boy of about seven years old, transfixed, staring at me with what was unmistakably the look of a child who knew what might be about to occur. The whole enterprise was turning out to be more threatening than I'd expected, but, although I had calmed down a great deal since leaving Woolverstone, the street kid from Fulham was taking over. I had reached the conscious decision that I didn't actually care what happened from this point on. I was all in.

'You must respect your grandfather; he is a good man.'

If I had learned anything as a child, it was how to insult in Neapolitan, and Nonno's lieutenants fumed as I told them the story of *girato le spalle*. Not because they believed me – they didn't – but because of the things I was saying within earshot of the man himself. I was still furious; this was a battle of wills and I'd returned to the overwhelmingly truculent 'take on all comers' version of me from school. I was also the undisputed centre of everybody's attention.

'You think you know him and call him a good man, but you know nothing,' I growled. When the incessant haranguing got too much, I took off the gloves. 'He, you and everybody else,' I shouted, sweeping my hand across the small crowd, 'can all go and FUCK YOUR MOTHERS!'

This purple flourish acted a little like the blast wave of an explosion. Through the gathered throng it went, and old men, women, children – I think even a priest had come from the church to investigate – tilted back simultaneously like cypress trees in its path. A chorused 'OHHHH!' rose up and then, for a moment, silence fell on the little piazza. The phrase, as I have imparted elsewhere, is as common as a *hello*, but such florid abuse, it seems, is not acceptable when addressed to an entire village, including mothers and their children. As the silence hung ominously for a moment, I sat with a smug face that looked a little like Robert De Niro's Al Capone in *The Untouchables* after he'd bludgeoned a miscreant to death with a baseball bat.

How do you like that?!

'*Disgraziato!*'

'*Mal educato!*'

'*Vergogna!*'

I glanced at the small boy again, and he was sniggering to himself. I enjoyed their disgust and disdain, but I hadn't quite worked out that I was providing evidence for what my grandfather had always said about Mum bringing us up badly. There were around eight of them surrounding me, mostly in their middle age, their anger palpable, but I was never concerned things would get physical, although there was more than a small possibility that the wrong person could have taken offence. If that had been the case, not even Nonno's exalted status would have protected me.

I remained at the table until Nonno could take it no more and, realising I wasn't going to be brought into line, or his dignity restored by a fawning apology, he went home, receiving soft pats on his back as he arose from the bench, each sympathiser turning to glare at me with disgust. Remarkably, my sense of belonging in that place was as strong as ever, despite the whole thing emerging from a rebuff. You see, it simply demonstrated that I had a reflected status there, and I'd never felt more at home.

Through that day I had become unspeakably furious with my grandfather, and I also saw how upset it had made my mother, who never dreamed he would do something so harsh when faced by my actual presence. She wasn't concerned for herself but for me. I had certainly been hurt by it, and in fact I don't think the incident or its significance to me and to Mum has ever really left me. I wouldn't say I idolised my Nonno, but he was important to us in so many ways. This was the very first real, tangible moment of rejection I had suffered, and it was one experienced at face-to-face proximity; but as the years passed I began to feel more remorseful about the whole affair and my role in embarrassing my grandfather, even though to this day I believe he deserved it.

Oddly – or perhaps not – I would have regular dreams about this event and, presumably as an exorcism, once wrote a short story about it. I had never before written a short story, and I don't think it is an especially good one, but it was a strange kind of catharsis, shaped around a Heaven Can Wait premise. The original plan was just to write a short story, entirely unrelated to me, but before long I couldn't help inserting small nuggets of facts into the narrative; by the time I'd finished, it was clearly about my relationship with Nonno and my father. It is full of events that clearly never happened, but the glue that binds it comes from the realities of my life and the clumps of real events I dropped into it. It reveals a lot about me, of course – and I *think* it forgives my grandfather – but once it was finished, I never had the dream again.

Beyond the fracas by the fig tree and our visit in 1991, when Nonno pretended it had never happened, in order to inveigle his son back into my mum's life, I had very few dealings with him again. Zio Matteo, who had curtailed his relationship with his father on account of his behaviour towards Mum, refused to believe my story and said his father would never have done such a thing. He had heard about the whole event in the village square and berated me for being so disrespectful.

In 1993, when I stood at my first wife's bedside as she gave birth to my daughter Leanora, the first words I uttered on seeing our new infant were: 'Oh my God, she looks like Nonno.' As I left the room an hour or so later, I got a phone call from Zio Matteo: Luigi Volpe, my grandfather, had just died.

LA FAMIGLIA PERILLO

There are always two sides to a story, and mine is no different.

The Volpe side of the family gave an alternative structure to my identity, inasmuch as many of them were in the UK and my early years in London were dunked in their and other immigrant Italians' lives and gatherings. Because of the difficulties around my parents' separation, my father's sisters, having settled in Somerset, remained largely estranged, without hostility, from us. Zio Matteo and his children were ever-present, and my father drifted in and out of the picture – mostly out. But Nonno Volpe was a huge figure in all of this, almost as if he were a giant who lived on a mountain but would occasionally visit our shore.

The Perillo family, despite their number, had not one single person living in the UK, and so it was our time spent in Italy that gave us the lived experiences that shaped my sense of where I was from. They would never visit the UK either, even when Mum offered to pay for them. Superstitious and fearful, most of them considered flying an absolute no-no. Suggest a train, and they would answer that trains crash. You also have to take a boat, and *they* sink. When the Channel Tunnel was opened, that was more unimaginably horrific than the ferry or flying.

The context is also important – Mum was from Montecorvino Pugliano, Dad from Montecorvino Rovella – two villages separated by five kilometres and a single mountain road but essentially the same place. Pugliano was more remote back then, and its inhabitants were poorer. So the Perillos and the

Volpes had always known each other, but it was an atmosphere of disengagement, resentment at what had been done to Mum, familial rupture and 'scandal'.

The Perillo family had their own difficulties, secrets, lies and some pretty savage history, too, but as a child I just saw a huge extended family. I'd never really experienced the attention of grandparents on Mum's side (and any attention from my father's parents was largely negative once I got beyond being a toddler). Mum didn't talk about her parents because I think her early life had been so difficult, but, as I write, there is so much I don't know. Mum retained some obvious bitterness towards her mother and father, but I cannot deny that these and other mysteries added to my own childish idea of myself as something a little 'windswept and interesting', as Billy Connolly might call it.

Mum was, however, to continue to be deeply devoted to her siblings (even the ones she sometimes disliked), and although her brother Isidoro was the eldest, she always struck me as the leader of the family. It was evident to me that she had an almost pathological desire to protect her brother Rolando and her youngest sister, Ines, baby of the family. Before Mum's dementia arrived, she would travel to Italy every year but never wanted to go home permanently. I asked her once if she would want to be buried in Italy, and her reply was emphatic: 'No! An' I donna wannabe be buried. I no wannabe puddina fucky 'ol.'

I think Mum had some very unhappy memories of Italy and would often talk about the things she valued about Britain as compared to her homeland. The current dismantling of those facets of the UK by extremist insurgents into our democratic process would have horrified her – maybe she might have contemplated going home if she were still here?

During the war she experienced some horrendous things, but my impression, without any real evidence up to this point, was that she got out of Dodge. She was always an Italian, though, and as far as I could tell was forever proud of that fact. My father, up to his death, spoke terrible English, but Mum, despite the colourful variations of words and her accent, learned to speak and read it very well. Occasionally, she once told me, she even had dreams in English, but I don't think she ever got to the point where she 'thought' in it.

Ferreting around in my memory demonstrates how little I actually know about Mum and her early life, and I sense something of a concerted effort by all those in her family to maintain a silence on particular aspects. I have snippets to fall back on, but it's not enough. Mum's personality, ferocious determination, her angst, the betrayals she suffered, how she approached life in England are all contributory factors both to how she coped and to how I am. Is that relevant to how I value my origins? Because I had ringside seats to her battles? Is what happened in her earlier life something identifiably a consequence of where she – and thus I – was from? Does it matter? I am starting off with the premise that it does. I have only one person left who may be able to tell me about Mum and her story, and that is Ines, her only surviving sibling who also 'fled' north to Florence at a youthful age.

I adore Ines – she is beautiful and funny and articulate. When we were young and visited Italy, it was very rare for us to see her, but she would occasionally be visiting Montecorvino. Mum had a sense of protective dedication to her, and that is how I knew her when I was younger – through Mum's usually emotional references to her. Later I did get to know Ines from visits to see her in Florence, and when she came and stayed with me in the UK (her fear of flying wasn't that profound), and I have kept in touch with her since. Ines had a difficult later life too, with a husband she separated from, but who left her in dire financial straits, before dying quite young. Ines is gentle, with a less agonised soul than many of her siblings, as far as I can tell. She smiles a lot and is abundantly affectionate and softly spoken, and one wonders if her early departure from her family enabled her to grow and develop in the way she did. Florence, being an acutely different kind of Italy from Montecorvino, would allow that.

I decided to go to Florence to visit her, to see if she would be happy, now everybody was gone, to tell me more about my mother.

I am very fond of my cousin Nunzia's son Vittorio (he is my cousin too, of course). He stands out among his family for having gone to university, in Salerno and then Trento, and at the time of writing has just become a doctor of philosophy in economics and management. This is a rare beast among the Perillo clan (although he takes his father's surname, Guida), and everybody is very proud of him. He also speaks very good English (another 'rare as a dodo' attribute). I suggested he joined me in Florence because the nature of my visit required a very thorough understanding of the facts I might learn. I could afford no misinterpretations, and my Italian is rough, dialect-riven and only patchily used. Ines is his great aunt, so he was pleased to agree to come down to Tuscany from Trento.

Also living in the north of the country is Ettore, the son of Zio Mario, Mum's youngest, but now deceased, brother. Ettore and his brothers Massimo and Fabio were regular playmates when we visited Italy. We loved their dad, and they had an apartment that backed directly on to a valley on the edge of Montecorvino which enjoyed spectacular views. Tragedy has struck the family, with one of Ettore's brothers taking his own life and the other dying young from disease. Their mother, also named Lidia, still talks to me via Facebook Messenger, and my heart has broken for her more than once.

I contacted Ettore, whom I haven't seen for decades now. I follow his life on social media – he and his husband Alberto have a life full of travel and joy, it seems, but I cannot imagine he is not a little bit broken by the experiences of recent years. I really would like to see him, so I ask if he would like to meet in Florence too, to see his aunt as well as reminisce with me. We had once hoped to cross paths in Sicily, where I like to go most summers, because, in a remarkable coincidence, it turned out that he and Alberto are very good friends with the owners of a small but spectacularly original restaurant in Donnalucata that we like to go to. We hadn't ever managed to time it right, so this reunion in Florence was a lovely thing to look forward to – but I worry it will be emotionally draining.

As if to remind me of the stakes, Vittorio, who was helping to plan things, asked me if Zia Ines knew her nephew Ettore was coming to join us in Florence. He was concerned that, with no knowledge of specific family history (he is a young man so is something of a feud novice), there might be, somewhere in the mists of time, a reason for Ines to be unwilling to see Ettore. 'I know how the Perillo family is, and I don't want to make a mistake or give her a bad surprise,' he said.

He needn't have worried.

***

A SMALL DIVERSION

I can't escape noticing, as I impart these facts, almost in passing, that my family is surrounded by sadness and tragedy. Means of death (other than the shooting in the face thing) are not unique to Italy, I get that. Nor is tragedy or sadness. Maybe this book is awakening me to the realisation that my Italian identity is merely the bauble hanging from naturally occurring misery?

Melancholia, like self-doubt, whispers in my ear about many things in my life. It reminds me of Mum and Matt, of separation, rejection, grief and relentless emotional demands that as a child (and some as an adult) I was ill-equipped for but nevertheless endured.

As I anticipated my Florence trip, I acknowledged the reality that the things I am trepidatious about *are* there, in Italy. The memories that might be evoked are there too, as are the people I would meet with, talk about and be reminded of. The joy and the pain all happened first in Italy. I was thinking of Ettore and our time as kids, his father and my mother together, his brothers' desperate fates. I was suffocating with a grief for our individual losses, how they intertwine, and was crumpling a bit. Without those numerous, crazy, heart-worn, frayed and bereft people, I would be nothing at all. I wouldn't talk the way I do, behave the way I do, eat and cook the way I do, speak and demonstrate in the way I do. Ines might tell me a huge story about my mother. She might not. But is it wrong to think its location is relevant?

I didn't set out to write a maudlin book. I *do* have happy memories, but I think I'm so far gone that they can't ever dominate a story. I tend to write 'live' and see where it takes me, so it isn't deliberate that I keep going down dark alleyways. 'Happy' is something I rarely feel – not in the way that I think most people define it, anyway. In the realm of memory, I recognise positive, enriching moments, and there are many of them in respect of my Italian experience, but 'happiness' and positivity are rare minerals. I suppose this diversion is designed to set out a context for all of this because it is probably important.

Let me give you an example, by way of one tiny vignette, of how, in middle age, I have become.

We love to visit Sicily, down in the south-east corner, where the gorgeous Baroque towns and wild countryside are, and although Sicily is an island, I certainly absorb it as a powerfully Italian place. On one visit, driving a large Mercedes car that the airport car rental office had mistakenly issued me, I was leaving a supermarket, coming on to the country road on my return to the place we stay. As you turn on to that road, there is an extraordinary view of the valley, sun beating down, all colour and light and preposterous beauty. At that very moment, on the luxurious, beefy stereo, a gloriously overwrought track emerged with the words, 'I think I just died and went to heaven.' It was the confluence of all these elements into one moment that did it – I felt a burst of euphoria, a feeling so alien that it was overwhelming. When you've had an adult life during which you cannot recall being more than mentally 'content', regardless of what is going on in it

– even the birth of children, love and marriage – anything above that baseline is dangerous, almost frightening territory.

'Ordinary' people go through lives of varying degrees of happiness or misery, but optimism, the regularity of cheerfulness and calm, is familiar and normal to them. It isn't to me. So when that burst of joy arrived in that car in Sicily, my brain immediately began to close it down until I got back to the comfort zone I knew, where blind optimism and happiness is a forbidden thing that will eventually be smashed on the rocks of one awful bloody disaster or another. So why go there in the first place? In his song 'Chalk Outlines', the musician and rapper Ren sums it up well by saying that one is afraid of accepting happiness because things often change again.

It is with this mindset that I am writing this book. It is not that I am searching for the anguish, I just keep stumbling across it; and the frequency with which I am doing so seems to serve the purpose of these efforts. Why am I the way I am? I have long since stopped fighting this mentality, and I accept that this is me, that it is all about just managing it. I do worry about its impact on my children. My fourteen-year-old daughter has learned to recognise when I am fighting back tears for no apparent reason or because of something on the television and I catch her looking sideways at me, fiercely scrutinising my face and eyes. We have a silent Mexican standoff where she is desperate for me not to crack, and I want to prove to her that I am not going to. But, on the other hand, I *do* want her to grow up being comfortable with and accepting of less happy periods in her life.

I have to confess that my eldest two have reached adulthood with a variety of undoubted consequences. My daughter Leonora suffered most, but she has an almost inhuman resilience that carried her through her teens and university years (although she may not have felt that way at the time). She once wrote an article that demonstrates my role in all of this; it is perceptive and telling, and I reproduce it below because I couldn't say it any better.

***

LEARNING TO LOOK UP

BY LEANORA VOLPE

Joni Mitchell's 'Chinese Cafe / Unchained Melody' is playing in Dad's steamed-up kitchen – he is giving me a lesson in good music and exemplary songwriting. We've listened to 'A Case of You', and to the whole of Wild Things Run Fast. *Now, Joni sings 'my child's a stranger…' Dad's face has crumpled, and I find myself half buried in his neck, embarrassed and close to tears myself.*

'Was it the song?' I ask after a minute or two, when he has composed himself.

'Maybe,' he says. 'Or maybe it's Matt. It just seems like I'm more susceptible to it recently.'

My Uncle Matteo's death in 2013 had a profound effect on my father who, as the closest brother to home and his closest living relative, shouldered the decision of turning off his life support in a silent intensive care unit. I remember that week well, during which I stayed unusually close to the phone, waiting for news or for Dad to call, needing to hear my, or anybody's, voice. Today I cautiously ask him if he is feeling depressed.

Dad describes the depth of the depression that surrounded the months after Matt's death, but that that isn't it; these days it's in a moment of poignancy or of sensory overload that he might feel a need to escape himself, which isn't depression, as such. I share my own impression of feeling suddenly, halfway through doing something that felt important or engaging, that it's pointless and mundane. We joke that our family has a hereditary tendency towards escapism, and how we are both afflicted by a sudden need to leave a crowded room.

***

An abiding memory of living with my father before the age of fourteen is his reign of silence from a computer chair, and of the hours he spent on the PC, pausing to silence me and my brother when our role-playing games became too boisterous. Sometimes he would compose jazz music, which he would then play to us in the car alongside Genesis and Puccini on the way to lunches at Nonna's in Fulham on Sundays, where I would revel in the noise of uncles debating and cursing in Italian at each other over the dining table. 'Vaffanculo!' my uncles would laugh over my head at my father, who would bite the side of his hand at them in jest.

These are memories I treasure, even though the unconventional parenting lent itself to raucous arguments with my mother after my brother and I had gone to bed, and often before. In spite of this, a bone-deep instinct knew that this half-stranger loved me, albeit differently from Mum, who took us to the shops and to the cinema at weekends and devoted seemingly endless energy to our childhoods, but less deliberate attention to the value of immaterial if infrequent moments of intimacy. I loved cosy Sunday afternoons with a new book and a bag of sweets, both of which I would devour with equal voracity. These seemingly mundane pleasures were punctuated with holidays in Turkey, Morocco, Tobago, where we all revelled in the excitement of boat trips and meals out, and Sprite from glass bottles, which with all their illicit novelty tasted better away from home.

Once we were taken to the mountains in southern Italy to meet our extended family. We ate enormous gelato cones in the cobbled streets of Sorrento, returning home with bronzed foreheads and sun-bleached wisps of hair at our temples. The presence of my dad in these episodes filled them with warmth, in part due to the sense that they were driven by an otherwise difficult to decipher family bond that I couldn't recognise in what I saw of my school friends families. At school I boasted about my family's relative exoticism, and peppered the playground with florid curses in Italian, not really knowing what they meant, but relishing the secret advantage of my teachers not knowing either. Dad would encourage me to write essays and read more challenging books, and fought dispassionate and indifferent teachers at school to do the same, but he didn't take us to the park or do crafts with us.

The selfishness of childhood made me resent his job, however; the long summer nights spent hosting guests at work, and the tired weekends spent recuperating in solitude. One evening in May I drifted into the kitchen from my room, where I had for months been spending entire evenings alone, talking to friends on MSN Messenger and descending inexorably into depression. My parents sat in the dark with glasses of wine. I can't remember if they were fighting. I stood in front of them and pulled up my sleeve to reveal four parallel cuts on my forearm, inflicted by a pair of craft scissors by my own left hand. All I felt was humiliation, less in the face of my mum than my dad, who I imagined to be profoundly disappointed in me. This was compounded by a need to shield him from my failure to be well and happy, an impulse which even in adulthood has never fully resolved.

Just days after this, my dad's presence in the household was interrupted by my parents' separation. He moved into a flat nearby, where I stayed with my brother on alternate weekends spent racked with guilt for my mum and sick with lethargic ennui that left its watermark on everything I did and saw. A psychologist at the children's mental-health clinic instructed me to scream at the top of my lungs to release my anger at my parents for divorcing and my resentment at Dad's new partner and their baby, and I could not, did not know what he was talking about, and couldn't locate such energetic emotions beneath the impenetrable fog, or understand the resentment I was supposed to feel.

And so it went for several years, with Mum bearing the brunt of my illness, which soured the air in her presence, but only slowed me down in his. The aim of the game was to look as functional as possible. At Dad's flat, I would eat dinner, grateful that he served salads doused in lemon juice, but occasionally lapsed into fits of anger at glugs of olive oil on spaghetti or on potatoes ready for roasting. In the evenings, with my brother safely occupied by the Xbox, we would stand in the kitchen chatting. Eventually, the conversation would turn to my eating, my low moods, my self-harm, and I would be speechless and unresponsive. He only just stopped short of begging me to be better, and I rarely opened up more than a crack.

'I thought you would be past this by now,' he would say. 'Why can't you just look up, at the sky?'

To me, his grief translated as impatience; to him, a fifteen-year-old's depression was teenage angst. Later, I would hear his suppressed sobs in the kitchen, and I would return, eyes down, to my books, knowing I was a stranger to my own father, but not knowing how to be any different.

I spent the next three years recuperating in Oxford, building a new life with the help of a new doctor and a heavy-handed medication regimen that came with its own downsides. I would see my parents occasionally and would in other weeks report on my progress or lack thereof. Never wanting to be the bearer of bad news, I was cautious when suggesting to my parents that my psychiatrist felt I should 'rusticate', or defer my place due to health concerns. I did my best not to come home too often out of fear of never making it back to college.

On short visits, Dad and I began to talk about depression and anxiety, and I started to share more honestly what was discussed in therapy, that I was finally learning what he meant when he asked me to look up on those nights in his kitchen – that I had so desperately needed the perspective of an entire world surrounding me, and some fresh air. Seeing my progress, Dad began to question whether my illness had been as profound as that of other sufferers he knew, but I didn't have the heart to explain to him how carefully I had curated my demeanour, and how I had saved my worst days for solitude.

No longer needing to spend so many hours trying to break down my façade, there was now room for him to nurture my maturing political interests, and for me to get to know him as more than just a stranger with whom small talk was difficult. We needled each other's differing stances on feminism, felt mutually outraged at an increasingly right-wing atmosphere, shared recipes for Neapolitan dishes and recommendations for films and songs. I began to miss him tremendously. I begin to take his advice from conversations about everything from my career to my love life.

* * *

This evening in a kitchen is no different from the cumulative hours in the cold with matching coffees, or boozy evenings at the theatre spent gradually unpicking the years we spent deeply misunderstanding each other. Many of our conversations combed over the dregs of my illness and my poor prognosis; and although I can't remember if I knew at the time that Dad recognised his own depression in mine, I recognise my own in his. I worry that the traits that we share now will reflect in my own parenting later in life, that I too will lack the energy or resilience to chaos that will be required for motherhood, but feel reassured these days that everything can be salvaged from rubble with time and healing, and that the flaws that alienated us have brought us together.

Today, what has kept us apart for my entire life – his instinct for solitude and disdain for noise, and my difficulty with expanding my world beyond the four walls of my bedroom – brings a moment of tenderness. This is, and always will be, a relief after my adolescent years of restrained silence. At the heart of it we are the same, and, for better or for worse, we share down to our very molecules a tendency towards melancholy. A decade later, I have never located the anger my psychologist talked about among the sense of incredible relief at having reached the end of those desperate years and my pride at my whole family having stitched itself into a new pattern.

Joni's voice interrupts a moment of silence. 'Nothing lasts,' she sings. Today the sentiment feels truer than ever.

* * *

I can't tell you of the pride I have in Leanora and her siblings. The references to her Italian heritage are so similar to the way I expressed my cultural connections as a youngster, and her recognition of my bond to Italy and how I fitted in with her perception of the place is deeply satisfying.

I can't pretend that it isn't painful to have my role revealed in her early suffering, but she's overcome it. My family has struggled through the fallout of whatever made me the way I am, but I'll put a little blame on Mum. A psychologist once told me I had 'learned anxiety' – and I'd learned it from Mum, who in any given scenario would often accelerate quickly to 'disaster' mode. He asked me a hypothetical question about the way I behaved towards my children when I perceived danger. How, he enquired, did I react if one of my children, when little, asked to walk along a small wall?

'I'd tell them it was impossible, and that if they did it they would fall off and break their leg, obviously. How else would I react? What would *you* do?'

He said he'd allow it and apply the condition that he had to hold their hand. I was so embarrassed.

116

THE DISCOVERIES IN FLORENCE

Where was I?

If there is a God, then Florence is His favourite city. The city certainly likes Him, with the Cattedrale di Santa Maria del Fiore – one of the world's greatest buildings – being its most generous dedication. Inside is a space that comes closest to what heaven might look like, and could probably convert the most fervent atheist to faith. I speak as one such fervent atheist who has wandered beneath its vast cupola and understood, for a moment, at least, how people succumb to religion in the first place. Devotional buildings in Italy go the full Monty, but in Florence's case, Santa Maria del Fiore's creators were so determined to consign every nook and cranny to majesty that they built a separate bell tower *and* baptistery, each of them capable of taking one's breath away. It has always amused me that the great dome of the cathedral was designed not by an architect but by the goldsmith Filippo Brunelleschi, who had entered a municipal competition to create the structure. The cathedral had been under construction for a hundred years, its original design including a vast dome that nobody actually knew how to create using existing architectural methods, yet still they displayed a model that continued to feature it, doggedly determined that there should be no change. In what seems like desperation, the city's leaders announced the competition; Brunelleschi entered and eventually ended up entirely redefining architecture. It was this dedication to bold public design and the rivalries that the competition ignited that

117

in turn sparked the creative conflagration of the Renaissance. I highly recommend Ross King's book *Brunelleschi's Dome: The Story of the Great Cathedral in Florence*, which places the whole affair into a beautifully detailed context.

As with Tuscany in general, Florence could be categorised as being in a different country from Campania, and whenever I go there I tend to feel this difference as locals raise eyebrows at my accent. In truth it is a city that belongs to the world, its status rendering its geography subordinate to the creativity that it gave birth to. I admire Florence for the casually dazzling way in which the city flaunts its importance to mankind; in response to the astonishment visitors experience, the city just shrugs its shoulders and says, 'Well, yeah, obvs.'

The period in history that Florence represents was always one of the things that as a child I would cite to elevate Italy above other countries. The Quattrocento and Renaissance had come to my attention early in life because I had an uncle who never stopped banging on about it, and I was soon doing the same. Imagine my pride when I discovered that my paternal grandfather had researched our family tree and got as far back as 1800 and a fellow called Michelangelo Volpe.

This journey is one of those rare occasions when I am visiting Italy with a purpose beyond that of sunshine, leisure, food and Negronis, but I am not sure what I will learn, or whether I will return with something troubling. I am trying to work out where to begin with Ines, what questions I should ask. I always sensed that Ines herself sought to leave Montecorvino as quickly as she could, but I am assuming that was for a malignant reason, when perhaps it was just adventurousness and restlessness. If, on the other hand, I am right about her departure, then I fear for what that means for Mum's story.

Arriving in Florence does for me what every arrival in Italy seems to do. I can only describe it as feeling very much at home, a sense of satisfaction derived from everything around me, even the little things, like the first perfect coffee, which at the terminal hall I rush to anoint my arrival with. When an Italian attempts to cut in front of me at the counter, I laugh to myself in knowing satisfaction. I laugh again as he dramatically feigns not to have realised what he'd done when I remonstrate with him. Then I *prance* out of the airport terminal to find a taxi, which in Florence is certainly a very different experience from Naples airport, where exiting the terminal doors smashes one full-on into chaos and ferocity. Both feel Italian, but Florence has a quietness and calm that I sometimes wish Naples had. My mini-altercation at the coffee counter could have turned into a knife fight in Naples.

The city is cold and damp on my arrival, which isn't doing much for the anxiety I am feeling about speaking to Ines. All of my previous visits to Florence have been in the spring or summer, when the marvellous architectural colours of the city are set against deep blue skies and bright sunshine. The winter drizzle and flat light lend a different perspective to the buildings; not being distracted by the *postcard view* of things, I wonder if I see more of the detail within them. I decide this is analogous with my reason for being here.

My hotel is on a street that terminates at the Ponte Vecchio. Leather merchants and elegant bookshops are a theme on the street, along with specialist art suppliers and jewellers, the latter presumably hoping to catch the gem buyers heading to the glorious *gioielli* paradise of the Old Bridge. I stroll along the road for the obligatory wander across the bridge, to gaze at the view of the Arno, but I'm driven away by a singer with a small speaker, mercilessly kicking the shit out of – before exquisitely murdering – '*Largo al factotum*'. Regardless, there is a three-deep gathering of admiring tourists around him, and I feel a sudden urge to leave because I'm worried that there will soon be another singer perching on the parapet of the bridge, to caterwaul a scarcely recognisable rendition of '*O mio babbino caro*' using an iPhone for accompaniment. Instagram has a lot to answer for, but the film *A Room with a View* has more. Such is the superficiality of popular social media culture. I'm being a bit of a snob.

I have some time to kill before I meet Vittorio, so I opt for a glass of wine at the enoteca Le Volpi e l'Uva. Even in gorgeous historical cities, I believe the best way to judge their mood and spirit is by drinking outside of a bar, but the choice of one called 'The Foxes and the Grape' is entirely fortuitous. A Twitter (X) follower has noticed where I am and, as they suggest I should visit it, I pass ten yards from its front door. Koestlerian synchronicity strikes again, and I text my cousin the location.

The enoteca is within a tiny unimportant courtyard off the Via de' Guicciardini and, even though the air is chilly and damp, chairs and tables adorned with small pretty lamps, all sitting beneath large umbrellas, invite al-fresco drinking. Inside, the enoteca is cramped and full of a variety of locals perched on stools, chatting noisily. Like every corner of Florence, the courtyard is like a painting full of small details, perfect proportions and colour. Even though I am impressed by them, in Florence you never get the sense that these beautiful things are done for effect. They just *are*.

Vittorio arrives, and I give him a bear hug. He still has his usual fervour for exploring his excellent English, and we are soon deep in conversation about his recent PhD and the travails of academic life. I know from the experience of friends in the UK that there is a nefariousness, and an almost vicious competitiveness, in academia throughout the world, but Vittorio brings his southern Italian cynicism and passion to it all. I am amazed again at the exception to the rule that he represents. His intellectual prowess is formidable, but he surprises me by saying how much he talks about me and *my* achievements to his academic colleagues. He is, he says, particularly partial to telling the story of my OBE (and if that particular facet of my life becomes a family fable, I expect that within ooh, say, forty years, I'll be a *member* of the royal family). I am sure he has looked into what the medal is and represents, so I explain, somewhat defensively, that I accepted it on behalf of my mother. As an immigrant she produced a generation that her host country recognises as having made a contribution of significance. That same country had issued her with a 'register of aliens' card when she'd arrived, so as an active political lefty, Vittorio understands and can forgive the dichotomy, appreciating my explanation that I consider the OBE to be the ultimate act of gatecrashing.

It is impossible to have anything but fully involved, animated conversations with Vittorio, be they about social sciences, his academic research or philosophical concepts, and I find myself feeling very proud of him. I conclude that, of all the Perillos and the Volpes combined, Vittorio, at the age of thirty, has achieved things not a single one of us has. We polish off a bottle or two of Sicilian red, and the cold and damp go entirely unnoticed.

Zia Ines, the reason for my visit, lives on Borgo dei Greci, a narrow street that joins Piazza della Signoria, home of Palazzo Vecchio, and Piazza di Santa Croce, where annually the violent spectacle of Calcio Storico is played out. Calcio Storico is treasured by Florentines, a continuation of savage sixteenth-century competition and tribalism to which the participants dedicate themselves fanatically. In Siena they have the Palio, in which horses and their riders take ninety seconds of death-defying risk, but in Calcio Storico, having chucked a ball in the air, fifty-four beefy men square up to each other and fight almost, it seems, to the death. Occasionally someone picks up the ball and throws it into a bin at either end of the square's sanded arena, but, if that happens, the ball carrier is targeted. It's bloody and powerful, a brutal contrast to the beautiful elegance of the surrounding buildings – including the spectacular Basilica of Santa Croce – that overlook the battlefield.

Ines, having made her move many decades ago, has therefore created a life at the very heart of one of the greatest cultural spaces on the planet. Vittorio and I meet her at the heavy front door of her building, and her smile is the same; her face is a little more aged, but she has a stylish haircut, as she ever did, and she looks fit and healthy, with a striking similarity to Mum. I hug her hard and wordlessly, and we laugh about how she may have shrunk a little since I last saw her. When my cousin Ettore arrives with his husband Alberto, forty years are put into our embrace, along with the memory and recognition of each of our brothers' deaths. We look at each other and don't need to speak. For the first time, I choke a little. Ettore hasn't seen his aunt Ines for decades, and their reunion gives me the satisfaction of knowing I had facilitated it; Alberto is happy to see these family moments because he knows what they mean to the man he is devoted to. When I messaged Ettore to see if he could meet me in Florence (they live in Milan), he had said he needed to check with work about time off. Almost instantly, Alberto messaged me separately to say: 'We will be there!' If Ettore had felt some trepidation, Alberto was clearly having none of it.

Lunch at the small trattoria opposite Ines's building is academic in many ways (though the wine and tagliata were memorable), and during lunch we all look at each other with a kind of warm gaze, catch up on so many things and take photographs. But everybody knows why I am there, and we know we will soon get to that nitty-gritty, upstairs in Ines's ancient little apartment, when family history will pass between us.

Ines was born when Mum was eighteen years old, so she doesn't recall a great deal of what Mum endured as a child or teenager, and I sense, too, that she is not familiar with much of what happened during Mum's early years because nobody has told her. Ines tells me much, but there is more she is not telling, and I believe there is no way, even if she knew everything, that she would share it. I am left to fill in gaps, make suppositions and take a detective's view, and I also realise that perhaps I know things she doesn't by way of being told them by other family members. And yet, although Ines remains matter of fact, through the course of conversation she begins to drop in astonishing stories I had never known, casting something of a new light on to many aspects of my mother's life. All of us sat riveted as we listened to each little bombshell land, asking her to repeat each story to be sure we'd heard correctly.

The originators of my mother and the family to which I became so attached, with whom I so strongly identified as a child, who provided the only real experience of a devoted extended family that I had, were Nicola Perillo and Anna Rega. Nicola was the man who handed me the sweet from his death bed, and Anna – or Annina (Little Anna) as everybody called her – was a mystery to me beyond what Mum had told me (and that wasn't much).

Ines was to reveal more of their story.

* * *

THE DEATH TELEGRAM

Nicola Perillo creamed back his hair, dressed himself in his only suit, his spry, wiry frame scarcely filling the shoulders of his tatty three-buttoned jacket, and rode with the funeral director on the high seat of his horse-drawn hearse. There would be time on this journey to contemplate how his behaviour and choices were now coming back to haunt him. From the peak of the mountain where his family lived, the hearse would process down the mountain road, through Montecorvino Rovella, to the town of Bellizzi, where it would turn left to run parallel with the coast on its way to Eboli.

Since arriving in Italy from Philadelphia, where he had been born in 1903, he'd done nothing spectacular with his life. His family had been driven back to Italy and their home town of Montecorvino Pugliano by the absence of the success they'd hoped to achieve by emigrating. Nicola had heard a rumour that his father had come home determined to find buried treasure associated with the local Nebulano Castle, but Nicola knew nothing of it and it had certainly never been found.

Hundreds of thousands of Italians had once made the pilgrimage to America, especially from the south, but not all managed to create sustainable, prosperous lives, and, for some, poverty in Italy seemed preferable to being poor in America. The Perillos had therefore made the long reverse trip across the Atlantic with disappointment. Nicola had his own fears, because he'd never spent time in Italy before arriving. The language was no barrier because in the family home in the US Italian was all they spoke, but his understanding of English was entirely worthless in Campania.

Now, in 1929, having once proselytised for the communists, Nicola had followed Benito Mussolini to the nationalist fascists and applauded their stance on the pointless indulgence of democracy and believed in the idea that classes could and should collaborate. The south of Italy had been forsaken by the north, abandoned to destitution, but Mussolini would solve this. Only that year he had granted Battipaglia, the town Nicola was now passing, independent municipality status. Nicola was sure it would grow to prosperity now. Things were looking up for Italy, but not for Nicola.

His indiscretion in getting a woman pregnant out of wedlock had now come to a tragic conclusion. From Eboli, where his lover Anna Rega lived, had come a grave telegram, sent by her brother: Anna had died giving birth. Nicola had avoided her for some time, and he knew the birth was imminent, but dirty secrets never stayed secret for long in the mountains of the Picentini. The thirteen kilometres to Eboli was a long enough journey for him to realise that his fecklessness now had the guilt of a death to go with the shame. He should come, said the telegram, to collect the body of the woman he'd deserted, and bury her.

He still wasn't sure if what he felt for Anna Rega was love or just a visceral passion. She was unorthodox, tiny in stature and very beautiful, as all of the Rega women were, but he'd never planned for their relationship to amount to much. From the moment he had met her, Anna was a lot of fun, never afraid of anybody and liked to get a little drunk. She had ferocious blue-grey eyes that penetrated whatever, or whoever, she looked at, and her family were tough, tenacious and never afraid to break a rule or piss on a convention if it meant making life a little easier. Anna's sister, Francesca, considered the most beautiful woman in Eboli, was a married prostitute whose lazy, hopeless husband lived happily off her labours. Nicola had been tempted by Anna's vivacity and beauty, but he was wise enough to want to avoid a fully fledged union because this was a family not to be messed with. Avoiding the reality of Anna's pregnancy had been easy enough for a while, even though he knew it would have to be faced eventually, but he'd decided to brazen it out and not marry Anna Rega. Now, unavoidably, at the age of twenty-six, he found himself facing not fatherhood or marriage, but a tragedy. The telegram had said nothing of the child's fate. Would he be burying two corpses? When he'd summoned the undertaker he'd mentioned only Anna, but the reality of the situation would become obvious if there was a baby to find a coffin for.

As he arrived at Anna's home in a narrow, dark street near to the church of Santa Maria Della Pietà and climbed down from the hearse, there were no people in the street holding a vigil or busily chatting and gossiping as is common when friends and relatives come for the traditional viewing of the body. He had expected to have to walk through a throng, all eyes on him in disapproval, a walk of shame, but there was nobody there. Perhaps, among the family and neighbours in Eboli, there was as much disgust with Anna as he expected there would be for him?

When he banged on the door of the house, Anna's brother answered and ushered him into the small living room. He'd gestured to the undertaker to wait outside, a command that rendered the *impresario di pompe funebri* indignant. '*Che cazz'?*' he muttered to himself.

Things seemed unusual inside, too, with no mourners, no family, no wailing mother, no rosaries, flowers or photos in frames beside them. How cruel, he thought, that Anna should be deprived of the traditional trappings of death and mourning. Will everybody pretend she hadn't existed? He knew what society thought of mothers who conceived out of wedlock. Near his own village was a high stone bridge and young women would be found beneath it, commonly believed to have thrown themselves from it. Everybody knew that not all of them were voluntary deaths and that some, scarcely women at all, would meet their end with developing babies in their bellies. The taboos he understood, but disregard for death was unusual.

Anna's brother had invited him in without uttering a word. There was just a silent exchange of glances, and her brother had looked briefly at his feet before nodding his head towards the double wooden doors that led to the large bedroom off the parlour. Nicola took a deep breath and steeled himself. He couldn't imagine the life drained from Anna's beautiful eyes, or what her strong, pretty face would look like, now that the spirit that animated it had vanished. He opened the door gingerly and could see daylight from the small window high in the wall spilling across the tiled floor. As the opening door revealed more of the room and the corner of the bed came into view, he paused and took another deep breath to calm his pounding heart, before pushing the door all the way open and lifting his eyes towards the dead woman's body.

'Oh, so NOW you fucking come?'

Sitting up in bed, clutching her new baby, Anna's fierce eyes were fixed unblinkingly on Nicola's face, condemning the cowardice that told her he had been more ready to visit her in death than in life, but also showing a glimmer of glee at having so comprehensively tricked him. It took Nicola a long, silent moment to process what he was seeing, and there was no relief at finding his lover alive. He whirred back through the possibilities and soon worked it out. Nicola knew the ways of Anna Rega, of her family and their boundless survival instincts. He'd thought her a little crazy from the moment he'd met her, and it wasn't a surprise that her brother had done what he was told, regardless of the cruelty of the fake telegram and the superstition that absolutely demanded that one should never, ever, tempt fate with a lie so enormous.

* * *

The baby was named Isidoro. I'm not sure if finding Anna alive made my grandfather love her more or less, but their story didn't end there, clearly. Maybe it was simply the case that he knew he should never again risk Anna's wrath, or just that he could not resist her physically, but neither of them learned their lesson, and two years later my mother, Lidia, was also born into illegitimacy. Eventually, no doubt overwhelmed by disapproval, Anna and Nicola arranged a combined service in which both children would be baptised and their parents would marry. They became a legitimate family, living in Pugliano, and went on to have seven children. Two would die as infants.

Ines, the final child to whom Anna gave birth, was unplanned and unexpected – an occurrence to which her parents had long since become accustomed. She came in 1949, eighteen years after my mother, and in the time between the death telegram and Ines's birth there had been catastrophic war, disease, famine, national and familial chaos and ceaseless poverty. Nonna Anna had become an alcoholic, pilfering wine from her husband's cupboard and topping up the bottles with water, and my mother bore the responsibility of looking after her siblings and running the home. She had not gone beyond elementary school, going instead to work in the tomato and tobacco fields to feed the family. So precarious were their lives that Nonna Anna's sister, Francesca, whom my mother took me to visit on the day my fingers were nearly chopped off in the door of the taxi, had offered to adopt the two girls of the family. Nonna Anna had thought it a good idea and agreed to let her daughters go to her sister, but Nonno Nicola forbade it. He may have done so because of Francesca's life as a prostitute or it was something else entirely. I do not know. My mother had of course left out telling me about Francesca's profession when she took me to meet her that day, but Ines explained that Francesca was a surrogate mother to them and adored my mum. I asked Ines why Francesca had made the offer – surely her life was incompatible with raising two girls? 'She had no children of her own,' she said. 'So she asked to take me and Lidia.'

I am tempted to see the proposal as an act of protection – though that doesn't appear to be something Ines countenances – and Nonna Anna's immediate agreement to the idea troubles me. Whatever the reasons for Francesca's request, it is clear their lives were dangerous and difficult.

Nonna Anna's children were all handsome and beautiful, and I can imagine Mum was much pursued, but when she met my father Francesco and fell in love with him, his own father, Luigi, the man who would later turn his back on me, expressly forbade him to have anything to do with her. The disapproval was so profound that he sent my father away for a period of time, to ensure they would not continue with the relationship. Bothered by my mother's heartbreak at the disappearance of her boyfriend, Nonna Anna took matters into her own hands.

***

THE SUIT

Anna Perillo (née Rega) had seen plenty of heartbreak and tragedy. It was enough anguish to last a lifetime. The final year of the war had been hell – so much death had stained Montecorvino, and her husband's continuing devotion to the fascists had imperilled her whole family. When the bombs stopped falling, the misery had endured. Even before the Germans arrived, she'd lost two infants to disease and had nearly lost her youngest son, Mario, to meningitis, but the old woman had saved him with her leeches. Her second living son, Rolando, was with the circus – it had broken her to allow him to go with them, but the regular stipend they sent her had been impossible to refuse. But now, poor Lidia, her eldest daughter, upon whom

Anna relied to look after the family when her drinking rendered her useless, was heartbroken.

Anna always felt some shame when she saw Lidia come home from the fields, brutalised by the work of picking tobacco and tomatoes, but still quietly going about doing the things Anna just couldn't do. Agricultural work begins before dawn in the summer, because by midday the heat is too much; by 1 p.m. Lidia would be home from the fields to cook whatever was left in the cupboard for lunch. It had got a little easier to get meat nowadays, and Lidia was a very good cook – she had mastered the elaborate lasagne of the region, with egg and salami, and also cooked a fine braciola – a speciality of Anna's, too. Her gnocchi needed work, but she certainly had skill in the kitchen.

When the food was eaten, off Lidia went, down to the fountains, to do the washing. When the hard scrubbing was done, Lidia would have to carry the wet load, balanced on her head in a large bucket, back up the steep path to the house in Pugliano. At least at the fountains, Lidia could be with her friends for an hour to gossip and laugh together as they plunged their hands into the freezing, spring-fed water. Anna knew she should be a better mother. Lidia worked like a horse and also looked after Ines, the baby of the family; in truth, Lidia behaved more like her mother than Anna ever did.

Anna shuddered to herself when she thought of how she almost lost Lidia during the war. Everybody was in danger when the Allied invasions began; Montecorvino had an airfield nearby and the invading forces tried very hard to take it. Either a shell would destroy a house and everybody in it, or the Germans would pull people into the square and shoot them in revenge for *partigiani* attacks. Acerno and Anna's home town of Eboli were almost destroyed in the fighting, and Anna was constantly concerned for her friends and family as the savagery surrounded them. After the Germans had left, Anna feared the reprisals, having heard about the terrible deaths in the north when revenge was taken against fascists and collaborators. But nobody came for Nicola.

Lidia's brush with death was as a consequence of dreadfully bad luck, but it was luck of a different kind that saved her. She was only twelve or thirteen when it happened. Everybody knew the Allies had landed at Salerno, but the fighting had not yet arrived in the mountains. The arrival of the Allies gave hope for an end to the Germans in the south, but there would be so much horror before that could be achieved – the Germans would not surrender. The fighting at Salerno and Battipaglia, a few miles away, could be heard, but Lidia had to go to the bakery for bread – they had to eat. With explosions in the distance, Lidia had crossed the small square in Pugliano to the little bakery and was inside talking to the old man when the detonations suddenly felt much closer, shaking the ground and buildings. Cowering behind the counter, the old man suddenly vanished into a cloud of plaster and stone. Lidia was thrown to the floor by the rush of rubble and stumbled out of the shop as people hurried to the scene and dragged her away. Climbing through the wreckage in the shop, her rescuers found the dead baker and, next to him, embedded in the floor, a large, unexploded shell. Anna wondered if the event was a sign that Lidia was blessed in some way. Superstitious locals came to the house to see Lidia, and Anna suspected it was to touch her so they themselves might receive just a bit of her fortune. Anna often thinks of that day and what futures would have been obliterated had things turned out differently. What lives may have never come to be if that shell had exploded?

Now the war was over and things were still hard, but Lidia had grown into a beautiful young woman. Plenty of the eligible – and several ineligible – men in Montecorvino were chasing after her. Everybody in the town would gather for the *passeggiata* in Rovella on the via Cappucin', and Lidia loved it because it was a few hours of just being a young, vivacious woman, walking arm in arm with her friends, when she could forget home life and its troubles. Anna had once, unseen by Lidia, watched her daughter laughing and joking with the boys, insulting and admonishing those who went too far. She was so elegant and made her poor clothes seem fashionable, mixing them with others borrowed from her friends. She looked, thought Anna, a little like a film star, with her sculpted, strong face and the same sharp, grey-blue eyes as her mother. Lidia deserved a greater stage than the via Cappucin', that was for sure.

Yet Lidia, despite having the pick of the town's bachelors, managed to choose badly and became infatuated with Francesco Volpe from Sant' Eustach', down in the lower part of Montecorvino Rovella. He was arrogant, not especially handsome, and his father Luigi was a council official who considered himself something of a town leader. Luigi Volpe had ordered his son to have nothing to do with Lidia when he discovered their relationship.

'Pah! Fuck him!' Anna thought. His son was nothing special and wasn't good enough for Lidia, anyway. The Volpes looked down their noses at Anna's family, and now the father, so horrified that his precious first-born son had become involved with a Perillo, had sent Francesco away, and nobody knew where, which meant Lidia was distraught, moping around the house, crying all the time. Anna wished her daughter would see that he would be no good for her; she begged her to understand the dangers of such a young man, but nothing she would do or say changed Lidia's mind or her feelings. Anna's only hope was to find out where Francesco was so that perhaps Lidia could at least write to him. In all truth, Anna was quite happy he was not around any longer and knew Lidia would get over it eventually. Maybe she'd choose better next time and find herself a better husband – maybe that nice boy Vito – but for now, she had to bring Lidia back to her right mind. Anna had lived on her wits all her life, and no bureaucrat was going to judge her daughter. Anna decided to confront Luigi Volpe in person.

There was one problem, however.

A woman could not be seen going to the house of the family whose son was seeking to affiance her daughter. These towns were so wrapped in traditions that a scandal could ensue from the smallest misdemeanour. Anna didn't care about that sort of thing, and her family had transgressed a hundred such rules and traditions, but she didn't want to embarrass Luigi Volpe or his wife by being seen walking to their home and banging on the door. A man, however, was perfectly entitled to do so, and as Nicola wasn't interested, Anna needed to be bold.

Nicola was a slight man, and his suit – the tatty one with a three-button front that he used to wear to Fascisti party meetings – would fit Anna. It was a little long in the leg and bunched up on top of the shoes she'd chosen from his wardrobe, but it didn't look preposterous. His shirt fitted well around her neck, especially when the tie was knotted in place, and his brimmed hat sat neatly on her bunched, scraped back hair. Anna thought to herself that if she kept her head down on the four-mile walk to Sant' Eustach', the hat would give enough disguise for her face. Mastering the walk was a concern, but wearing the heavy shoes gave her a naturally masculine gait, and she was sure she'd get away with it. She took a few moments to work out how to button the jacket. Nicola only ever used the middle button of the three, although Anna had always felt it should be fully buttoned, but few men ever did that. Best stick to convention, she thought.

The first three miles along the mountain road from Pugliano to Rovella were incident-free; few people walked that road. Her exasperation at the rules that made this farrago necessary was mitigated a little by the excitement she felt. The difficulty came when she entered the crossroads in the centre of Montecorvino Rovella and had to walk across the central piazza, before taking the long hill down into Sant' Eustach, at the bottom of which sat the church. From there it was a stone's throw to the Volpe house, but that was the danger zone, where people could see a person approaching a home.

In the piazza in Rovella, from the corner of her eye, Anna saw many people she knew: if they had recognised her she didn't know how she would explain the situation to them. She felt butterflies in her stomach and, encouraged by her rebelliousness, even considered taking a seat at the small corner bar and ordering a coffee, just to see if she could get away with it. She thought better of it.

As it happened, nobody was paying much attention and common sense told her that, although she might feel everybody was looking at her, in reality they weren't. Everybody in Montecorvino was going somewhere with a purpose, because all of them had pressing things to achieve – such as feeding their families. Very few people strolled around aimlessly, paying attention to anything and everything; they were head down, brows furrowed and focused. This was probably a consequence of the war, when the Germans became occupiers, and people did not want to draw attention to themselves. It did occur to Anna that perhaps nobody would have noticed her calling on the Volpes as herself anyway, but that thought was very quickly pinched from her mind. 'Oh, they'd notice, all right!'

All she had to do was remain incognito until she eventually got the chance to bang on the Volpe door. When that moment came and Luigi Volpe opened it, Anna pushed past him into the small stone-walled parlour and took off her hat. Luigi was aghast, recognising Anna immediately.

'What in God's name are you doing, woman?! Why are you dressed like that?'

Anna simply raised her eyebrows to him questioningly, and Luigi understood. He knew how crazy Anna Rega was, even before she married a Perillo, and while this was quite the stunt, nothing really surprised him.

'Why do you think I am here?' Anna's eyes were fierce.

Luigi was already feeling irritated and indignant at this woman's temerity, but he knew why she was there.

'My son is not to have anything to do with that daughter of yours. Everybody knows about the Perillos and the Regas. And your sister, for that matter,' Luigi sneered.

'Well, Signor Volpe, we are in agreement. I don't want my daughter to have anything to do with your son either – he is nothing special. But my daughter thinks he is, and she is heartbroken. You and I will probably get what we want eventually, but for now I am not prepared to see Lidia so unhappy. Where is your son?'

Anna was pointing her finger at him, and her eyes were aflame.

'I am not obliged to tell you that. And I am not *going* to tell you, either. He is far enough away,' said Luigi, 'and I am sorry your daughter is unhappy, but I am sure she will get over it.'

The arrogance of the man, thought Anna. 'I bet your son doesn't agree with you, does he?'

Luigi laughed a little. 'My son will do what he is told, signora.'

Anna could tell Luigi Volpe was never going to reveal his son's whereabouts, and felt a little defeated. She didn't have the energy to continue demanding an answer to her questions; she wasn't actually too unhappy about the separation, and Luigi's pomposity suggested he'd stand on principle until the cows came home. She considered whether she was *really* most bothered by the Volpes thinking themselves better than her family.

Luigi Volpe had a reputation in town and garnered respect, although not quite as much as he thought. He'd been a prisoner of war in Russia for years, and just turned up one day, thin and gaunt like a ghost. He worked for the Commune, so had a finger in every pie in town, which gave him a self-satisfied air of superiority. Luigi Volpe, everybody knew, was never wrong. He certainly wouldn't have enjoyed Anna's demanding tone, because nobody spoke to him that way.

'Let me tell you something, Luigi Volpe,' she hissed. 'Your son is a waster. I have seen his type – I have seen him playing cards and gambling. You think the sun shines from his arsehole, but he will never be good for my daughter. Perhaps we will both live to see that, perhaps we won't, but I also know that neither of us can stop this right now.'

Luigi had no answer. It wasn't that he feared Anna, but he knew she didn't fear him, and that was almost the same. He could dominate his son, but he could never dominate tiny Annina. Having issued her final tirade, Anna placed the hat back on to her head, opened the front door, looked out briefly to see if the coast was clear and began the long, uphill walk to Pugliano.

* * *

Francesco had been in the north of Italy, probably doing his National Service, and eventually returned. He and my mother made plans to elope to Britain, a country advertising itself to Italian citizenry as a destination of dreams and opportunity. In reality, it needed labour to help recover from the war, and Italians took the chance in their thousands, disembarking from the boats or trains and stepping into a still-hostile atmosphere. After a secret, quicky marriage, at the age of twenty-four, Lidia had begun a journey that would eventually provide more sorrow and struggle than anybody deserved.

Throughout her life, my mother would refer to her little sister Ines in terms that always betrayed a great deal of pain, and it must have been devastating for her to leave her six-year-old sibling, whom she'd cared for and protected since she had been born. I cannot say for certain if it was her desperation to escape or her infatuation with my father that made her abandon Ines to the care of an alcoholic mother and a seemingly ailing father, but I know she never got over the sense of guilt she felt. Ines would thereafter be effectively raised by the teachers at her elementary school until she became old enough to look after herself.

The story of Nonna Anna and her unorthodox family is one that eventually resonated down through her children, who without exception bore the scars of their family's dysfunction. Nunzia, daughter of Rolando, remembers Nonna Anna unkindly. When Nonno Nicola died, she recalls being taken to her grandparents' home to participate in the traditional viewing of the deceased. Sitting next to the body of Nicola was Anna, calmly eating chocolates – behaviour that suggested to Nunzia that her grief wasn't as profound as it should have been. Like me, Nunzia will have by now understood the impact of her grandparents on her own father, Rolando, whose life and behaviour must have been set within him by the things he experienced.

***

THE FUNGAIOLO

Even in the dawn light of the forest, Rolando could see them, standing proud at the foot of the pine tree, their creamy stems, tall and thin in bunches, topped by the small brown caps. Pioppino mushrooms were popular at market: for frying in garlic, or to turn them into a soup with peas and pancetta, their nutty, flowery taste irresistible. He cut a few bunches and placed them into his basket and knew that at least today he'd make some money. But Rolando is an expert *fungaiolo*, famed for his ability to identify and find the edible mushrooms of the region without killing anybody by mistake, and he expects to find more. He's lucky – in Campania, the mushroom season is long: from spring until December one could find them among the pines. Finferlo are as common as grass but always desired, or russula, fat, meaty and perfect for the flame grill, or pratolio, porcino and so many others. Rolando doesn't even know all the names, but when he takes his full basket to the market to sell to stallholders, he can explain how best to cook them, what herbs suit them, how to roast, fry, barbecue or boil them. More importantly, he can describe how to prepare those species that retain the potential for poisoning: boil them, remove the scum from the water and so on.

If truth be told, Rolando's need to descend from the forests into Montecorvino to sell his assiduously harvested goods is the worst part of his job. Up in the forests is where he feels happiest, alone with nature and his thoughts, in the cooler air with the pungent smells and relative dampness. The heat of the coming day is signalled early, and he always makes sure he has his tattered straw hat on his head, to protect him from the sun of the open glades and exposed hillsides that take him up to the hunting ground. The anger that often courses through Rolando's veins is absent in the forest, and his desire for a drink is reduced too. If only he could stay up here for ever.

Rolando knows his powerful body is still his best chance of paid employment. He is a Hercules of a man, even in his forties. His older brother Isidoro is responsible for organising the annual Ferragosto events, so there are always a couple of weeks of heaving equipment around for him. There is a lot of building going on, too, and labourers are in demand, but Rolando has the heart of an artist, a singer and a poet. He wishes he had fewer muscles because perhaps he would be taken more seriously, but who would want to hear him sing, read his poetry or respect the heartfelt musings of this seemingly simple man of the land?

There was a time when Rolando experienced fame and adoration, but it was for his physical prowess and came after misery and years of feeling abandoned and homeless, wandering the country with the circus. As a child, Rolando was always athletic and strong – he could balance and walk on his hands with ease, climb and fling himself acrobatically into any challenge without even thinking about it. When the Circo Fratelli Zavatta came to town, he and his friends would excitedly run around the encampment trying to emulate the acrobats and the most glamorous stars of all, the trapeze artists.

When he saw an old man from the circus talking to his mother one day, he couldn't imagine that she would allow the circus to take him away to train with them. He was only a small boy, maybe nine or ten years old. He knew it would bring some money to the family, and he just wanted to be at home, but he still felt the excitement of every show, of every town and the glamour he believed the circus represented. Within a short time, he was performing with the acrobat troupe, somersaulting his way to the peak of a pyramid of bodies, wrapped in a silk costume and with makeup on his eyes. By his mid-teens, his body was developed and strong, he was a fine acrobat and he began to train on the trapeze. His strength made him a potential catcher, and his mesmerising good looks did not go unnoticed by the circus owners. As a creative soul, Rolando didn't just want to be the brute catching all the bodies that were allowed to express *their* finesse as they flew through the air towards him. He insisted he be allowed to develop his own solo swing show, to take his place on the bill as an individual, to become a star in his own right. And he had achieved that much at least.

Eventually he had become sick of his unsettled life. Now he has four children of his own and poverty rules their lives; he still has his muscles and his physique. His eldest sister, Lidia, is visiting again from England; her four boys always insist on hanging from his biceps together, two on each arm.

Rolando loves Lidia, and every time she comes she brings with her clothes for everybody. Rolando's children are beside themselves with the T-shirts carrying English phrases, and Rolando likes the vests that don't tighten on his arms and shoulders too much. Lidia and her boys are staying with him, and she has helped out with a little money, too. She is good company for Rolando's wife, Anna, cooking with her and gossiping, but he fears what Anna might tell her sometimes, which means he often stays away until the food is on the table. Lidia always lectures Rolando about his behaviour and his drinking, his absence and his occasional violence. His big sister has always been the real matriarch of the family, standing in for their mother, and Rolando knew how much his being sent away with the circus had affected her because Lidia was all heart and tears.

Even though he can sense her anger with him, Lidia can still make Rolando feel safe again, his brave, selfless sister who had changed so much, yet understands him better than anybody. Maybe if she had stayed in Montecorvino, her support and presence may have diverted the course of his life, but she seems totally unwilling, even at the depths of her broken marriage, to return home. Now she comes with her boys, who love to be with their cousins and who in turn revel in the fact that they have relatives from a far-off land. Rolando can see, through her children, how strong Lidia has been and how well she has survived her husband's desertion, but he still hates him. He remembers how their mother had always known Francesco Volpe would be no good for her, but Lidia wouldn't listen and has suffered so much pain. It was only Lidia's pleading that stopped Rolando kicking her husband to death. She deserves more, and Rolando can never find it within himself to fight back or argue when she takes him to task – she has a way of making him feel deeply ashamed, but he knows she is right.

Rolando hates how he has become, the way he takes his dark moods out on his family sometimes, his frequent retreat into the bottle. Today, in the forests where he feels more like himself, Rolando knows the darkness is descending upon him again. He worries about Ferruccio, his son, who like all young boys is in danger of mixing with the local delinquents. He worries about his girls Nunzia, Lidia and Ines, who all fear him a little but still have the goodness to see the side of him that he can sometimes show them – his humour, his love of singing, his big, powerful presence. But Rolando has come to accept that his course is now set, and he sees no way of escaping the demons that haunt him. He'll just have to find a way through the rest of his life.

Was his gloominess all about the memories of the neglect, the fact his parents were prepared to send him away, that both his sisters left Montecorvino for better lives elsewhere? Rolando was poor, too, and he often felt he was clinging on desperately, hiding behind his big character and the charm of humour, the flourish of a funny story and his reputation. Some people fear him a little, and so do his family, yet most people consider him to be a gentle giant. That just isn't the whole truth.

'Pah, fuck it,' he thought. 'It is what it is.'

With his basket now full of multicoloured fruits of the forest, Rolando pops open his cigar box, fixes one to his bottom lip, lights it and begins the long walk down into the town. He is a well-known sight in Montecorvino, with his baggy trousers, tatty straw hat and vest, carrying his basket full of culinary gold, and everybody greets him as he passes. Rolando rarely says much in response – a slight smile with the cigar still attached to his lip, or a nod. Occasionally people stop him and look through his basket and ask to buy some of the funghi before they get to the market stall. Rolando will acquiesce for the right price, but rarely are the buyers generous or realistic enough – and few of them actually know what it is that they want to buy, or how to cook it. Better to keep the stall-holder dealers happy with the cream of the crop.

As he turns on to Via Cappucin', where the market stalls line up twice a week, he can see his nephew Michael, Lidia's youngest son, approaching him with Ferruccio. When Lidia comes, her children make the most of their new surroundings and play in the mountains or ride scooters. Michael is about ten, wearing a bright yellow T-shirt, skipping along the road. The boys have sticks in hand and large, empty tomato tins. Ferruccio and Michael are close, and both are loud and instinctively confrontational.

'Zio Rolando!' Michael shouts.

The boy seems to worship Rolando and is excited to meet him on the street. Rolando knows what is coming next, and Michael flexes both his biceps in the pose of a bodybuilder and expects Rolando to reciprocate. He does, and as ever, Michael feels Rolando's muscles, his face full of wonder and amazement. Then he grabs hold with both hands, and Rolando lifts him effortlessly from the ground with his bicep as the boy squeals with excitement.

'Where are you off to?' Rolando asks Ferruccio.

'Catching lizards, Papa,' he replies.

Rolando looks down at his nephew, winks and summons him close.

'Michele,' whispers Rolando conspiratorially, glancing from side to side, 'whatever you do, don't grab them by the tail.'

* * *

I am able to stitch together the scraps of these stories and understand better what my mother's early life was like, and I am tempted to call it operatic. Her own mother's propensity for dramatic gesture and her reliance on the bottle would determine that Mum's life was one of serving others, of taking care of people, watching out for them. The betrayal by my father when they got to the UK would have been a blow she could scarcely have expected and most certainly didn't deserve. When it came, she was condemned to live her life fearing, and seeking to divert, the potential dangers we faced. Considering the things I know about her life in Italy, as well as those I can only speculate on, it is indisputable that my mother was a traumatised soul. I know the horrors of the war stayed with her, and the perilous demands of 1930s and 1940s Italy were tacked on to the peculiar behaviour of her parents, including the violence of her father. The resilience she showed right up to her death is astonishing within the context of a life that was cruel to her until the end, but she is remembered by all her nieces and nephews as the woman who brought them clothes, who stood up to their fathers and defended them. She is almost worshipped.

The Italian socio-religious system that operated during my mother's childhood and before, when her own mother breached the golden rules of wedlock and propriety, set her and her family's lives on a particular path. I never lived by those rules, and neither did Mum when she was in England, but the dimensions of that culture were unquestionably part of the course, not only of her life, but of mine too. The constructs that demanded uncompromising adherence meant that those in her family who transgressed were condemned to stay together when perhaps they shouldn't have, or were silent and unyielding when today we might talk about it. Secrets and lies are caustic and painful; we lock them away and families split, incubating grudges and animosity.

The naturally emotional disposition of my Italian family stood out from those of my friends, and I found it bizarre that families might not argue and scream at each other; that gratuitous, loud and empty conflict wasn't as common to others as it was to me. But demonstrable affection, as plain to see as it could be, was built on a bedrock of pain, intense individualism, addiction and often violence. As a child, these people were a fairy tale to me, but now, with age and reflection, I can see the cracks that the sugar-coating hid. Mum's superpower was navigating her way through all the tribulations as war and famine struck Italy, and then again in England when poverty, language barriers, prejudice and the plain, simple heartlessness of her husband put the hurdles in front of her.

It strikes me that few, if any, of the children of Nonna Anna had much of what we would recognise as a childhood – the very real truth is that I have no history but *their* history. That *is* where I come from; my name, my experiences, the outrageous stories that I am able to tell you. I am as much a product of the society that produced Mum as she is. This much I learned from Ines.

Florence, then, has delivered knowledge of a different kind. I have learned about Mum's beginnings, the remarkable resilience of her early life and the unconventional nature of her own extended family. My cousin Ettore has also found the experience emotionally punishing, and Vittorio, Anna and Nicola's great-grandson, has come to realise his place in all of this, too.

As I prepare to leave Florence, I have no doubt of my right to associate with Italy – the love the people here have for me, the profundity of their own memories of my mother and our visits that punctuated their lives. They mean something to me, but I also mean something to them. How can I possibly accept the assertion that I am English because that's where I was born, when I am looking at a giant fresco of my family story? What has England ever delivered to me that is equivalent to this monumental extended family and the experiences I'd had with them? I have no history in the UK, only a lived life.

Vittorio and I meet with Ines outside the Palazzo Vecchio to say goodbye. Without warning, Ines begins to weep. I have many times bid her farewell, and never have I seen this kind of emotion. It isn't just a tearful goodbye: she is viscerally distraught, unable to control her grief or speak. '*Non piangere, Zia, non piangere,*' I beg. She is tiny in stature, and I want to scoop her up as she buries her face in my chest, trying to stop herself falling apart. I don't know why, but I suddenly feel as though I too am abandoning her. She is by no means alone; one of her sons and his family live in the apartment next door to her, so I know she is loved and protected. But I still feel as though I am taking something away from her that she needs. Perhaps it is my connection to her beloved sister – she is the last of the generation. Is she worried, I wonder, that this might be the last time she will ever see me? She tears herself from me and begins to walk back across the square to her home, still crying, looking back at us.

'I will bring everybody, all my family, to see you soon, Zia. I promise,' I say.

She nods, fighting to compose herself, and I feel desperate. And guilty. I have brought us together, three offspring of her siblings, and we have evoked memories of her life, of her parents, brothers and sister. At the airport, haunted by the pain in Ines's face, I fight my upset, hiding behind a fixed, clenched expression and a face mask, but that irreversible moment still arrives, when the warm tears leak on to my cheek. I have rarely felt so overwhelmed.

AND SO...?

In exploring the lives of these Italians I call family and scrutinising Italy and its ways, I realise that I have said as much about the state of the UK as I have anything else. Actually, on reflection, as I write, the political atmosphere triggers simultaneous feelings of alarm, pessimism and mourning. That doesn't mean I have changed the way I feel about my heritage, and neither does it suggest I consider Italy, which has a far-right government at the time of writing, to be in any way more virtuous than the country in which I have lived all my life (indeed, it was the virtues that my mother felt Italy lacked that created her loyalty to, and belief in, the UK).

I always had an admiration for what Britain represented – and provided – and understood the stability it stood for, regardless of the political party in charge. That has now eroded to a point of real concern, for the medium-term future, at least, and I wonder how low the encroachment of the far-right will drag the country socially. I don't feel particularly confident that a Labour government would change much, since it appears, in its current form, to have chosen a path of pandering to the uncomfortable views the extremists have encouraged parts of Britain to celebrate and express.

I think I realise that I just am what I am, and *English* is not it. Feeling Italian didn't give me my moral compass or belief in decency – if anything the British did that, which is why I feel so outraged at what is occurring now. The irony is that Italy probably wouldn't laud me for anything I have achieved in the way the UK has, but it would certainly have claimed me were I to have become an international-standard sportsman. However, even though the feeling of displacement I have experienced throughout my life is something I have never held against this country, its intensification in recent years must be laid at its feet.

I have portrayed Italy through the eyes of a child, who then grew into an adult without really adapting to his surroundings. The Italy I describe has many a wonderful thing, but not all second-generation Italians feel the way I do. Recently, as I walked home from an errand, I bumped into a woman whose father had been a family friend, from a village one along from Montecorvino, and she was voicing to me how she has an abrasive relationship with Italy, predicated on the sexism she has experienced there. This book and my own family stories demonstrate that Italy has a social dark side that is more savage than the UK's; for all the *dolce* there is equal *amaro*. And it isn't Britain's fault that it doesn't have the precise landscape, climate, language, history, food, wines, architecture, etc., that Italy does – it has its own version of those things. All that Italy offers became an intrinsic part of my self-perception, but it was also from a distance, a table heaving with goodies that I could see, but wasn't sitting at, except on special occasions.

The story one sets out to tell is not always the tale that eventually gets told, and this book is no different. I thought there was something scientifically and socially important to say about my predicament – there may well still be – but I clearly lack the talent, patience or, ultimately, the desire to explore it in any real, empirical detail. I can assure you that any perspicacity present in this volume is probably fortuitous.

Having realised my shortcomings in this regard, I naturally lurched off into the lives of my grandparents, uncles and cousins, because I realised they have stories that deserve telling, lives that should be recognised, because I have come to understand the part these historical episodes play in my own journey. How could I possibly refute this influence? There is a direct line from Nonna

Anna's negligence to my mother's pathological desire to protect her own children. It is why Mum had a fist fight in Fulham Court with a woman who traduced her son. It is why in turn, having absorbed her angst, I worry furiously about my own kids. When my mother tied yellow ribbons around the pull chain of the toilet cistern whenever Matt was in prison, it could probably be linked directly to the departure of Rolando with the circus.

Every family can chart a course of events through history to their own current lives, and mine just happens to have taken place in an extraordinarily historic Mediterranean landscape, with customs and traditions that are very different from those in Britain. I don't have to try to quantify it more than that, and I am perfectly sure *now* of why I think of myself in the way that I do. I'm a product of a process, and in fact it is clear that I personally matter little to the course of the story, because while I may have always felt the tentacles of a dysfunctional family tightening around me, I am still, when all is said and done, just a witness. Or a victim? I wouldn't run my flag up the latter's flagpole with much enthusiasm, but I am undoubtedly damaged goods. The social conditions of my childhood and the extended family environment I experienced have made me insecure in so many ways – I was obsessed with losing Mum as a child, even if she had only gone next door for a moment of calm, to escape the behaviour of us boys. I vividly remember the anguish I felt, thinking she had gone for ever.

Writing more of my mother's story was important, and yet I still believe I haven't written quite enough. It is easy to caricature my mother – and I do a little in these pages – but she was a titan, as resilient and dedicated as anybody I know. She was wily and smart, too, but what characterised her above all else was her heart. She didn't always do or say the right things – who does? – but she did them fearlessly, with a florid profanity and a dogged, relentless courage. Not all of her sons survived her, but Matt, who died in 2013 from a brain bleed, made it to an age that at one point had seemed impossible, and Mum, not just luck, was the reason he achieved that. Mum's dementia meant she never knew of his passing.

I have written about my mother's death from dementia and how at the time I felt desperate that I had never really *told* her how much I loved and admired her, or that she had succeeded in ways she might never have felt she had. She instinctively knew of our affection for her, but was that enough? It haunted me then, and haunts me still, but in her eulogy I said:

> *You had a fulfilling, worthwhile life, as noble, as distinguished and as glorious as any other. Your struggle was not in vain. You did it, Mum, you made it.*

It was too late, of course, and as the Neapolitans say, *'Mamma, denare e ggiuventù se chiagneno quanno nun ce stanno cchiù.'* People will cry for their mother, money and youth, but only after they are all gone.

My daughter Leanora, who, along with her brother Gianluca, expresses her feelings creatively (she through poetry and Gianluca through music and song), recognised my failings in this regard – how my brothers and I never really appreciated Mum's sacrifice and overwhelming dedication. On her Nonna's death, Leanora wrote a poem and, again, I reproduce her work below, which encapsulates Mum's decline and recognises with unerring accuracy what her life – and her nationality – represented.

> *Flaming June is on the wall as always*
> *When we arrive on Sunday morning*
> *Espresso on the squat coffee table as always*
> *Aubergine smoking in the pan as always,*
> *Treats in children's pockets as always,*
> *But you should have realised she was fading*
> *When she forgot to wash the soap out of her hair this time.*
> *And did you realise she was fading when she*
> *Left bowls of broccoli for the cat, still*

None the wiser to his name and always
Trying to let him out the door?
Raw sausages at teatime, cold soup
Milk in the wardrobe —
These were ours to keep.
But you should have realised she was fading
When she called to ask the way home.
You should have known she didn't only mean her flat —
That the only way back to herself was you.
And even when she knew your names by heart
She'd call you by your three brothers' before she got to yours
Her way of taking stock, making sure
You were all still there, her boys,
A roll call in Neapolitan swing,
Quiet forgetfulness bound by the remembering
Of all who surrounded her —
And those who didn't —
As if to boast her way of bringing a family together.
So when the chant of Italian folk music,
Louis Prima singing to his Angelina fades
Into a nocturnal blue and orange flicker, mutter
Of infomercials, tiredness draining
Out into the gutter and I at fifteen
Not understanding why I couldn't sleep.
A sunlamp at the bedside,
Last-ditch reminder that the sky is blue
Told us everything we already knew
That she was the one *who painted it blue.*
And now that her final whisper of her fierce defence of family,
Soft murmur — 'Oh Mamma' — has
Left our ears for the last time,
I know it feels like not even you can remember the sound of her voice.
It is up to you to carry on singing the songs she wrote
Because she wrote them for you
They were always for you.

It is a poem that runs me through whenever I read it (as I write this paragraph, I can scarcely see the screen), but I hope, in some small way, that this book and the telling of her life is obedience to my daughter's final command.

Losing Mum severed a connecting thread to Italy, but, through social media and more frequent visits, my links to the family are stronger than ever. More recently, my son Gianluca returned to Montecorvino with me, having not been since he was a small boy. As a grown man, he relished the chaos and emotional banditry of the family get-togethers and was as transfixed as I had always been by the conversations of his cousins in broad dialect. The apple doesn't fall far from the tree.

This volume set out to tell you something about identity and culture, but while I hope it has given you some insight, I accept that all I may have done is added vivid colour to a line drawing. In my bolshier moments, I would make the case that the rise in the UK opera audience's appetite for late-nineteenth and early-twentieth-century Italian works is a direct consequence of the extraordinary, lavishly dysfunctional and tragic lives of my family. If I could make that stick, I would die a happy man.

Whatever.

I don't know how many children of immigrants feel the way I do, but their parents and grandparents have undoubtedly coloured in their own vibrant little part of the UK's historical and cultural map. And now, with new wars, more refugees, growing diversity, we will see a new generation of people adding their histories. But they will be even less welcome than my mother was – and she had been invited. Some people fail to understand why communities find safety and comfort together; it is what my mother and other Italians did when they first arrived, and we criticise people for that today, too. They must integrate, we say, as we chuck bricks through their windows, intimidate and frighten them by standing and chanting outside the hotels we put them in, and call them 'swarms' or 'invasions'.

It is tragic that many of those seeking refuge in the UK are doing so because of the reputation the country has for the things it once did so well, but shamefully, because of an over-promoted phalanx of horrendous people, have either long since ceased to be or are in the process of being dismantled. Even more shamefully, those very same vandals continue to parade their patriotism, even as they wreck the nation.

As I write, the loudest, most hostile government voices that rise in opposition to refugees are themselves children of immigrants. Furious and frustrated that her flagship policy of shipping refugees to Rwanda had been thwarted by the High Court – or 'lefty lawyers' as she always refers to them – the Home Secretary, Suella Braverman, a fervent Brexiter, made an angry statement in response.

'The British people will no longer indulge the polite fiction that we have a duty to support everyone in the world who is fleeing persecution.'

Her argument for the policy of instantly deporting refugees who landed in Britain via boats had always been that refugees were, in reality, just economic migrants. However, her rage meant the façade was breached and we saw the depths of her animosity. That such words should come from a British Home Secretary is unfathomable.

This almost daily rhetoric affects anybody who has immigrant roots and alternative cultural identities, because you do not have to be a *refugee* to feel the reflected heat of a relentless assault on the 'other'. Italy is the instrument that forms the process of my evolving identity, but it could be any culture. That process is not to be scoffed at, and should be understood, but it becomes dangerous when some cultural identities are placed lower on the totem pole when expressed within the environment of a different host. When a host invites that alternative culture to exist only on its terms (integrate or else!) then one's sense of *difference* is often reinforced. You may reasonably conclude that a host culture takes primacy (certainly in terms of laws and behaviours), and

I would probably agree with you, but that primacy does not naturally confer supremacy. As I have said, in Italy's case, the British allow themselves to admire much of its culture, and I don't feel *rejected* by the UK. Those of certain other nationalities, faiths or skin colour will have had a completely different experience. My selfhood was largely abstract, an adjunct to life, but over the years I have been moved by my inner discomfort to see ways I might become a target of the racists if push came to shove. In recent years the hands on my back have felt a little heavier.

In a recent conversation on Twitter (X), I was discussing this feeling of attachment to Italy and, despite voicing the issue in terms similar to those I use in this book, there were some who automatically viewed my position as being one of hostility to the UK. To them it is a binary issue: to identify and value your familial heritage is not permissible if you were born and/ or raised here. I'm wrong, they say, to 'feel' the way I do; they find it hard to understand, and the only conclusion they seem able to arrive at is that I 'hate' Britain. Explaining that my life, particularly in my youth, has been immersed in Italian culture, and that ninety-nine per cent of my extended family live in Italy, has been met by a number of people with dismissive irritation. If I say something critical of the British government, or a social reality in the UK, there will be someone who will make an Italian comparison, as if assuming I would approve of racism, for example, in Italy, but not in the UK.

Throughout my life I have often been subjected to loyalty tests by those who see only malice in my naturally occurring sense of identity. There are two principal challenges put to me: who would I fight for if there was a war between the UK and Italy, and why don't I go and live there? The first question is insufferably childish, illustrates the nature of nationalism and is an impossible question to answer (and I usually ignore it because it is so ridiculous). The second is a more reasonable enquiry, especially as I often say how at home I feel in Italy. It is really very simple − I don't want to live there, and I don't have to live there to identify with it. I have had fifty or so years living in the UK, and my life is here now, as are my children. As I related earlier in this book, there is so much about Italy that infuriates and is chaotic, but there are places I probably could live that are less guilty of this, like Florence or the lakes, picture-book versions of the country that mask much of the precariousness that the part of Italy I know best suffers from. But when the day comes that I have had enough of Britain, it is more likely I will go and live in Finland or Norway, for example, where I would nevertheless continue to feel Italian.

A book like this is rarely anything but a self-examination, an attempt to understand and put into words what one has never been able – or felt compelled – to do previously. As it has progressed, I have learned more about my own history and its impact on me, and how my view of Britain is being changed by the British themselves. The hostility grows towards people born both here and abroad, but hate is also finding targets among a variety of diverse people, not just foreigners. Slowly, the ire of the extremists is shifting on to the same old victims it always focused on, with some new ones they'd previously missed. Transgenderism enrages them, but then we have attacks on feminism, too, and any form of equality is called 'woke' – but the commentators who find fertile ground for their hate in a particular arena exploit the upset they cause in order to align themselves with, and garner support from, people they would ordinarily despise. Far-right TV presenters who attack transpeople claim to do so in support of women, but they don't care about women, either; they perpetuate the traditional roles of women, begin hostile narratives on abortion, ignore violence against women, attack single mothers, never argue against the still persistent pay gaps and, in general, rubbish the concerns of women. An MP who came to office as part of the 2019 election's Red Wall 'Brexit' intake recently mocked an activist woman tweeter because she mentioned how she'd needed the services of the Samaritans – so mental health is a target, too. The Pride Flag and Pride Month in particular are constantly attacked, and there are worrying signs of a return to the conflation of diverse sexualities with paedophilia. It is all so dreadfully false, mendacious and manipulative. Disabled people, poor people, striking workers (the list is endless) – all come in for the far-right treatment, and they maintain a constant poking of the population, to annoy, to anger, to mislead and seem to truly believe that a country can exist peacefully with such endless rancour. This is what Brexit ignited.

Maybe, by the time this book hits the shelves, things will have begun to change under a different government, but I am not optimistic. Above all else, what I hope readers will better understand is why culturally diverse people continue to feel put-upon, are suspicious and sensitive and want others around them to hate less. We want people to appreciate and understand the value and delicacy of difference, and maybe just learn to sit quietly and watch the world pass by in peace.

We too have stories to tell.

* * *

A LONG ROAD

'The train leaves Victoria at 8 a.m., Mrs Volpe – try to be there a little early,' said the travel agent, who had assiduously studied his printed European train timetables, worked out all the connections and booked, by telephone, the many elements of Lidia's urgent journey to Montecorvino in southern Italy. He had then, from his desk, produced (miraculously, as far as Lidia was concerned) ticket books for the French railways, Italian railways and the ferry company, writing them all by hand through carbon-copy paper.

His little travel agency sat next to the butcher's shop on the Goldhawk Road, and Lidia had never before had reason to use him, but she was ever so glad she had now. He was kind and decent, explaining carefully the things Lidia didn't understand,

and he hadn't resorted to impatience or speaking slowly and loudly, as so many other people did. She'd arrived anxious and tearful in the agency but was met with empathy and kindness; she expected neither in her usual interactions, so this had put her more at ease.

Lidia's English was good, but the terminology of travel, of trains and transfers, confused her a little, so the agent went into great detail about how she should get across Paris from the Gare du Nord to the Gare de Lyon, where the trains to Milan and Rome departed. She couldn't even imagine herself finding the right bus and it taking her through the fabled streets of that great city, but the travel agent eased her fears a little: 'I've done it lots of times, Mrs Volpe, and it is very easy. Just make sure you get on the Number 20 bus.' He drew her a little diagram of the station so she would get to the right stop. Lidia was already emotional about the journey, and this man had sensed it. She wanted to hug and kiss him for his kindness, and she resolved to bring a dish of lasagne for him and his staff when she returned.

Lidia was also worried about the ferry. It brought back memories of the time Francesco, her now estranged husband, had thought it funny to hang her then two-year-old son Matteo over the railing of the high upper deck by his feet. Lidia had almost fainted with fear, but this time it was only Lidia and her youngest son Michael making the trip. He was just two and a half, so she would be sure to sit inside on the crossing, and there would be no excited walks on deck to look at the sea. He was a boisterous child – he would be safer inside, even if the floors were awash with vomit from a rough crossing.

As the final details were arranged and Lidia handed over the bundle of cash in return for an envelope full of tickets, leaflets and hand-drawn diagrams, she suddenly felt so weary and empty. A telegram had arrived two days earlier from her mother, Anna, telling her that her father, Nicola, was at death's door, and that she should get to Italy as soon as possible. Lidia remembered the story of Anna's famous death announcement telegram to her father, and how her mother would laugh about it to annoy and ridicule him. He always responded with, 'But I came, didn't I?' This time, the telegram was real, and Lidia had cried when it arrived, even though she still felt a deep anger for her father that meant she had even contemplated not going to see him. The cost of this trip took most of her savings, and, because she was on her own with four boys, she needed every penny for the basics in life. But something very powerful made her want to go home to be with him, and so her reluctance didn't last long. It would be good, she decided, to see her mother and siblings, too, even in a moment of such sadness.

It was just over two years since her husband Francesco had left her for the last time. He had done it before, and had even produced a son with the other woman, whose name Lidia cannot bring herself to speak and who had been a teenage friend. She'd needed somewhere to stay when she first arrived in England, and even though they had little space for her, Lidia and Francesco took her in, because that's just what everybody in the Italian community did – they helped each other and stuck together. Soon, Francesco's behaviour had begun to raise suspicions in Lidia's mind, and she became convinced he was having an affair. A rage always grew in her when she thought of how she spent hours crying and talking to this woman, who sought to reassure Lidia it was nothing to worry about, yet all the time...

Under their own roof.

Puttana!

Francesco eventually returned, begging for another chance, and in no time at all Lidia had become pregnant with Michael; she just couldn't find a way to resist trying again. She had hope, but maybe she just had no choice, and deep down she knew what was coming. Heartbreak was the overwhelming experience of his first betrayals, but when he left again, on Christmas Day, with Michael a mere six months old, Lidia felt fear.

Real, deep fear. How would she cope with four young children on her own, with only one meagre income? That morning, Lidia had demanded that her brother-in-law Matteo drive her to the flat where she knew Francesco would be found. Screaming up at the window from the street, with her six-month-old child in her arms, on Christmas Day, was as low a moment as Lidia had ever suffered, but it also put something else into her: steel and determination that she would never be humiliated and rejected again. When Francesco came down to the street, no doubt to beat Lidia, Matteo had stood between them and warned his brother firmly against touching her.

That was in the past, and Lidia had recovered somewhat, but now she has other family matters to face and to try to exorcise.

* * *

As the train to Dover began to pull away from Victoria, Lidia was already missing her three other boys. The Tully family, neighbours in Woodstock Grove, were looking after Luigi, Matteo and Sergio, because Lidia couldn't afford to take them or remove them from school. The Tullys were good people, and Woodstock Grove, although little more than a slum where few had much at all, had provided Lidia with support and friendship, despite there being some who obviously detested immigrants. Gracie upstairs would sometimes babysit the kids until Lidia returned from her work, and occasionally Old Man Lacy would give her one of the chickens he bred in his back yard – slaughtered and cleaned, of course. Gracie's dog had probably given the boys ringworm – according to the doctor – but Lidia couldn't hold that against her. She was an elderly widow with a lovely heart, and she adored the children, but she couldn't manage all three for a week, which is why the Tullys had offered to take them.

Lidia had twenty-four hours of travel ahead of her, and she prayed Michael would be calm. She couldn't afford a cabin bed, so she would need to sleep sitting in an ordinary seat for the long leg from Paris to Rome, and would place Michael tightly between her and the window, strapping him to her wrist with a belt once he had nodded off because she was terrified someone would take him as they slept.

Lidia often felt anxious those days, especially where her children were concerned. One of the most amazing things England offered was a universal vaccination programme, so she at least didn't have to worry about diphtheria, cholera, smallpox or polio as she had in Italy, but her need to work constantly in order to keep their heads above water required her to take risks and let them be a bit more independent. They play on the building sites, the parks and streets around Woodstock Grove, and she forever carried an image in her mind of a policeman knocking on her door to tell her some awful news about one of them. The knot in her stomach was constant.

Lidia often felt overwhelmed when she thought of the way in which she has been treated – by her husband, by the world, by fate itself – but she didn't want to feel sorry for herself, so she took every small job she could find, because she refused to claim benefits. Above all, she wanted to prove to that pig of a husband that she didn't need him. The Italians she knew who had come to England visited her, or she went to them, and they all ate big meals and reminisced about their time together back home. Her brother-in-law, Matteo, had been a constant presence with his growing family, refusing to speak to his brother for deserting his children. Lidia wasn't alone, and while none in her community had wealth or could help much with material things, she felt lucky to have the job as a cook at Brook Green Day nursery, which also accepted Michael into the baby room. She loved being around all those children and the young women who looked after them.

Lidia could sometimes force herself to believe she was laying the foundations for a better life, even if the mice and damp in Woodstock Grove suggested otherwise. Only the other evening she had found a mouse crawling over Michael as he slept in his cot, but she had put her name down on the council housing list for a proper home, to replace the two-room basement slum she lived in. Although her social worker had told her it would be a while before one with enough bedrooms would become available, better times at least felt *possible*, because she believed with all her heart that Britain wouldn't let her fall into destitution as she might back home. Social services had taken an interest in the family – a lone young woman with four small children is the kind of situation they always take an interest in – and her social worker had helped Lidia fill in forms for things like bus passes for the kids, carefully explaining and simplifying more complicated documents for her. She was sometimes afraid of her social worker because she had heard of children being removed from families who couldn't cope. The kids were always clean, even though she had to wash them in the kitchen sink, with the door of the switched-on oven open for warmth; and if she had time, she would boil water for the steel bathtub – but that was rare, perhaps just once a month. All of the children were prone to hurt themselves, though, from playing in the street; there was the time Luigi came home with a dart in his chest. Matteo was frequently at the hospital with cuts and other injuries. Every time she took him to be stitched up, she watched the doctors intently, to see if they might be discussing her child's wounds in a suspicious fashion. Again, the fear would grip her, but even though there might be stern questions from the doctors at the hospital, nobody came for her kids. Lidia thought her obvious attachment to her children demonstrated that she herself would never hurt them, but she knew deep in her soul that her children were always at risk, no matter how fiercely she protected them.

But here, sitting on the train with Michael scribbling on paper with crayons, not half as excited by France rushing past the window as he had at first been, she wasn't sure how she would react when she saw her father. She was excited for her family to meet her youngest son for the first time, but it depressed her that it was imminent death that brought them together. Michael had not been intended, and naturally Francesco had laid the blame for yet another child at *her* door, but Lidia was a fierce mother and couldn't think of anything she was better at, though at the age of thirty-seven she was physically and emotionally exhausted. She tried desperately to imagine a time when that wouldn't be so.

* * *

Isidoro was there to meet Lidia at Salerno station in his rickety old Fiat, and she gasped at how like their father he was becoming with age. He had a little of the same brusqueness, too, but seeing him made her begin to weep, which confused Michael, who watched her intently, perhaps trying to work out what this man meant to his mother. He had seen her cry before. Many times.

'How is Mamma?'

Isidoro just shrugged and tutted gently – traditional Campanian body language that meant 'as you would expect', or 'what do you think?' But Lidia didn't know what to expect of her mother or what her reaction would be, and she even thought that her mother might be relieved her husband was at the end of his life, that she wouldn't have to deal with him or compete with him any longer. Isidoro looked at Michael, sitting on his mother's lap, and reached across to tweak his cheek. The child pulled away and kept staring at him as Isidoro laughed.

'*Bello!*' he said.

As they arrived in Montecorvino, driving along Via Cappucin', before taking the left turn on to the steep road up to Pugliano, Lidia was struck by the new buildings that had gone up since she was last there. They were mostly moderate apartment blocks, stacked across the valley-side opposite the Via Cappucin', but it was unmistakably a time of renewal for the region. The old houses were still there, and her family lived in those, but who knew where all of this rebuilding would lead them? Her other siblings – Mario, Rolando and Ines – would all be at the house, taking turns to nurse Nicola and supporting their mother, and

Isidoro said their father had very little time so they should go straight there. Lidia began to weep again, and Michael turned to look at her.

Once Isidoro had parked, Lidia took her son by the hand and led him up the steep little hill into the small courtyard beneath the Perillo house. As she walked, she could feel the eyes of people in their doorways on her, and one or two called her name in greeting. Lidia's stomach knot had tightened and grown on the journey from Salerno, and she felt sick. At the door of her childhood home was her mother Anna, her siblings behind her in the parlour, looking intently at Lidia as she approached. Michael pulled a little on her hand and tried to stop walking, but she gently coaxed him forward. '*Andiamo*, Michele, *andiamo*. It's OK.'

Anna reached out and cupped Lidia's face in her hands and kissed her on both cheeks. Then her brothers and sister greeted her in the same way. Each took a turn to grasp a reluctant Michael and give him a kiss, but Rolando blew a raspberry into his neck and Michael giggled.

'He will be glad to see you,' whispered Anna, 'and the baby. How sweet he is!'

Anna said he could go at any moment, but he was conscious and able to speak a little. Lidia was becoming overwhelmed and was beginning to regret bringing Michael; she worried how all this grieving might affect him. Would he remember any of this? Leading Michael into her father's dark bedroom, Lidia could scarcely breathe as she pushed the door slowly and the corner of the bed came into view. She paused and tried to steady her heartbeat before pushing through fully to look at her father. Nicola Perillo, the fervent fascist of old, the angry man who drank too much, was shrivelled into the mattress, his arms over the covers, a crucifix above his head on the tall wall. Lidia looked at him through her tears, and he smiled back painfully. Then Nicola looked at Michael, who was staring intently at him, overawed by the darkness, the height of the room and the heavy atmosphere, and signalled to Lidia to open the drawer of the bedside table. In it she found some sweets, wrapped in gold foil, and Nicola took one from her and offered it to Michael, stretching out his withered hand effortfully.

'Here, take it, *bambino*.' At first Michael hid behind the leg of his mother, but eventually stepped out and took the sweet from his grandfather's hand.

Lidia had so much she wanted to say to her father but didn't know how to say it, or even what the point of it would be, and Nicola could hardly speak more than a few words in any case. She was pleased he had met his grandson before the end. Lidia always felt her parents had an innate love for their children but had difficulty expressing it. She had slaved to serve this man hand and foot when she was little more than a child herself, and his tenderness towards Michael had surprised her. She decided words were unnecessary, and she sat on the chair beside the bed and took Michael on to her lap. She clasped her father's hand in hers and sat silently with him.

Nicola died that night. He just drifted away with the doctor holding a stethoscope to his chest, with his children standing huddled together behind the doctor. The next day, people came to the house to view his body, with Anna sitting dutifully as sentinel beside the bed, welcoming visitors into the room. As she did so, she occasionally took a chocolate from a small box to chew or to hand to children visiting with parents.

Funerals in Italy take place the day after death, if possible, and so Lidia was able to be there with her siblings and many other family members and friends. Nicola was buried in the community cemetery on the road to the coast – when passing it, drivers always crossed themselves if they had family members in there – and afterwards Lidia felt desperate to sit down with her mother to talk. She missed her mother and considered how she could have done with the support of her family in recent years. Anna was hard and uncompromising on so many things, but Lidia still acknowledged her strength and wisdom from time to time.

'I told you,' said Anna, 'that Francesco Volpe would be no good for you, didn't I?'

'Mamma, please, not now,' replied Lidia.

'He has left you with four children, Lidia. You know you don't need him, right? He just wants a slave to look after him and wash his clothes and cook his food.'

Lidia was angry that her mother had chosen now to rub salt in her wounds, but she knew she was right, and that just depressed her more. When Francesco and Lidia had at first started dating, Anna was furious she had chosen a Volpe, a family she thought arrogant. Lidia never understood her mother's animosity, why she said he was useless and pointless and a gambler, but she understood now, and although that realisation had come too late, at least Lidia had four beautiful children to show for the catastrophe of her marriage.

'Mamma, I know I don't need him. I am never forgiving him again. So don't worry,' said Lidia.

'Are you sure about that, Lidia?' Anna laughed cynically as she said it.

Rolando, who was listening to them speak, became angry. 'I will kick his arse from here to Acerno if I see him,' he said.

Lidia really had moved on from Francesco's desertion, had decided he'd left her for the last time, and it was understandable that, having taken him back before, her family would worry she might do it again. But she didn't want Francesco to have the satisfaction of getting one of the Perillos put in jail.

'Rolando,' Lidia pleaded, 'I want you to promise me you will not go near him if you see him when he comes here. OK?'

Rolando loved his big sister and wanted to protect her, to punish her husband, but he had to agree to her wishes. In any case, he was worried he might even kill Francesco.

'How is life in London, Lidia?' asked Anna.

It was impossible for Lidia to describe to her mother just how it was she was living. She could explain the work she was always doing, the financial troubles, the relentless drudgery of survival, but it was harder for her to explain the environment in which all of this was taking place. London was so completely different from Montecorvino, the scale of a big city, the nature of the English, the society she was navigating. Lidia was glad she had learned the language, had found a community of sorts in Woodstock Grove and was always surrounded by Italians, so to set her mother's mind at rest, she explained only the positive things to her. Even though she was poor by English standards, Lidia had enough sense to realise she was infinitely better off than her family still living in Italy.

'Just remember, Lidia,' said Anna, 'you can always come home. Your children are young enough. They will cope.'

'That's not going to happen, Mamma. I don't want to come back,' replied Lidia with steel in her voice. Anna dropped the conversation because she knew why her daughter didn't want to live her life in Montecorvino Pugliano. Lidia herself couldn't see how that would improve things because in London she had regular work in a job with a pension, and she felt that returning to Italy would be an admission of failure, one she knew her mother would revel in a little.

'England does good things for people like me Mamma. The children are fed at school, I am waiting for a better house. The English are honest. Life is OK.'

'Does Francesco give you money?' Anna asked, even though she knew what the answer to her question would be before Lidia explained that he had been ordered by the court to pay her a weekly maintenance, but he never did.

'Mamma, will *you* be OK?'

Anna paused and smiled at Lidia. 'Oh yes,' she said.

Lidia would spend a few more days in Pugliano. It was good to see her family and friends, and her grief over her father lifted a little. But she began to miss her children desperately and looked forward to getting back to Woodstock Grove. Italy wasn't where she wanted to be, because so much had happened there, and she had become used to her home in England. She could always visit – maybe soon she could afford to fly instead of taking the long twenty-four-hour train journey. Lidia was proud of herself for what she had achieved, what she had come through. Leaving for England had been exciting and almost felt safe when she had done it with her husband, when they could face challenges together, but now the fear had replaced the certainty and security of a cohesive family unit.

She would face it; she would pull through the tough times. She looked at Michael, his innocence yet to be sullied by life, and wondered what would become of him and his brothers, who had their entire lives ahead of them but whom she would need to be strong for, to fight for. She would *always* fight. She knew she could do it, and she had no idea what life had planned for her, either, but she was sure of one thing: it would be a very long, hard, lonely road she would have to travel. For strength, and perhaps as a resolution to herself, she thought of one of her favourite songs:

You weep only if no one sees,
and you cry out only if no one hears.

ACKNOWLEDGMENTS

The nature of a memoir requires its author to delve into the past, into things that have remained unexplored for many years. It's a little like swimming out into a lake, knowing the water beneath you is growing deeper and worrying about what creatures might meet you at the surface. The fear, in this context, is not entirely irrational; inevitably, monsters *will* appear.

The consequences of this singular, anxious focus include ending up in something of a private bubble, so I would like to thank the many people who were prepared to tell me when I'd forgotten the reader in all of this, particularly Helen Hawkins and Professor Alexandra Wilson. Much gratitude, too, to those who were gracious enough to encourage me to keep going.

Love and thanks to my wife Sally and to my children, Leanora, Gianluca and Fiora.

Most of all, I want to celebrate my mother, Lidia – who really was the best parent I could have hoped for – and the family she delivered me into, which has, for better or for worse, and as I hope this book will illustrate, made me who I am today.

WITH DEEPEST THANKS TO SUPPORTERS

OF THIS BOOK

Richard Hayter

Oliver Gooch
John Grumbar
Martin Kramer
John McEachen

Johane Ansell
Vittorio Guida
Jennifer Kettlewell
Sally Lykiardopulo
Christina Maxwell
Brett Newman
David Moss
Stephen Louis Parperis
Allison Palmer-Challis
Maria Thomas
Harriet Tupper

Gillian Bromfield
Alice Connew
Adam Porges
John Savournin

FAMILY TREE

Not all family members are listed – only those who feature.

Nicola Perillo & Anna Rega
(my maternal grandparents)

<u>Isidoro</u>	<u>Lidia</u> *(Mum)*	<u>Rolando</u>	<u>Mario</u>	<u>Ines</u>
Nicola	Luigi *(Lou)*	Nunzia *(Vittorio's mother)*	Ettore	
Pasquale	Matteo	Ferruccio	Massimo	
Mario	Sergio	Lidia	Fabio	
Giovanni	Michael *(me)*	Ines		
Rita				
Antonella				
Clementina				
Anna Maria				

Luigi Volpe
(my paternal grandfather)

Francesco *(my father)*
Matteo

ABOUT THE AUTHOR

Michael Volpe OBE is a writer and opera company leader best known for founding Opera Holland Park. Born to an Italian immigrant family in London, Michael attended Woolverstone Hall school, where he explored his love of music and drama – an experience he wrote about in his memoir *Noisy at the Wrong Times* (included by the *Sunday Times* in its '100 Biographies To Love' list). In 1996 he founded Opera Holland Park, and became a specialist in late Italian opera. He retired from Holland Park in 2020, and was awarded an OBE for services to opera. He lives in London.

@NOISYVOLPE 📷 🐦 @NOISYMV